PRAISE FOR
JOHNNY CAME LATELY

"*JOHNNY CAME LATELY* WILL HAVE FANS LINING UP IN THE BOOKSTORES. It is a reader's buffet—truly something for everyone. . . . De Cordova is a masterful storyteller, and his book is filled with anecdotes . . . a first-person view of one of America's favorite entertainers by one of the industry's most entertaining writers. . . . THERE IS ONLY ONE PROBLEM WITH THIS BOOK—IT'S TOO SHORT."

—*Boston Herald*

"A GREAT READ . . . DE CORDOVA IS A WONDERFUL STORYTELLER AND YOU WILL NOT WANT TO PUT THIS ONE DOWN."

—Larry King, *USA Today*

"It's never a dull party if de Cordova is there—he is witty, elegant and charming, and his book reflects this."

—Gene Kelly

"De Cordova's book is probably as good a look as we've had about the backstage workings of the show, and it's a close, fond. . . . look at Carson."

—*Los Angeles Times*

(more . . .)

JOHNNY CAME LATELY

An Autobiography
by
FRED DE CORDOVA

EXECUTIVE PRODUCER OF
THE TONIGHT SHOW

POCKET BOOKS

New York   London   Toronto   Sydney   Tokyo

POCKET BOOKS, a division of Simon & Schuster Inc.
1230 Avenue of the Americas, New York, NY 10020

Dedicated to so many people
with whom I've worked and played—
and, most of all, to Janet,
who has made my life such a happy one.

The author wishes to thank *The Tonight Show* and the writers Ray Siller, Kevin Mulholland, Andrew Nicholls, and Darrell Vickers for permission to reprint "Excerpts from Fred's Diary," "Public Service Announcements," and "Jokes Between the States."

Contents

CONTENTS

Foreword

There are a number of valid reasons for the writing and the publishing of an autobiography: intense interest by the Public in the strange and devious life of the author; his or her desire, finally, to tell the Truth and, by so doing, strike back at all the detractors who tried so hard to destroy him; and, most important of all, the knowledge that there is a vast, impatient group of readers who really care with whom he or she ate, spoke, and slept. None of the above is the reason for this autobiography.

Of course, every author devoutly desires that the Reader will enjoy his writing, and that is, of course, my foremost wish. But I find it vital to point out that I am not to blame if you don't enjoy yourself. You should realize that I was minding my own business, delighted at being highly overpaid every week of the year (and damn near making income equal outgo) as the executive producer of *The Tonight Show Starring Johnny Carson,* when, to settle an argument with one of the writers on our staff, I mentioned that I could prove my point by showing him an entry in one of my diaries.

Yes, I've kept a diary every day (or the morning after if the events of the evening were a bit too strenuous) since January 1, 1932. Don't bother to count—that's fifty-five years of personal gratification or shame. And on that January day, I wasn't exactly a child—but what do you care how old I am!

Maybe you do. I'm seventy-six years of age. I've had rather a remarkable run of success on Broadway and in Hollywood, and television has been my pal for almost twenty-five years. I'm in semi-splendid physical condition, I shoot eighteen holes of golf in the low eighties, I drink a good deal of vodka every day, and all my friends tell me I smoke to excess.

Anyhow, the writer I told about the diary told the other writers on our staff and the trouble started.

I'm sure you understand that writing comedy material for *The Tonight Show* (no, not everything Johnny says is something he thought of that morning in the shower) isn't exactly the easiest job in the world. Just check your friends and cronies and see how many of them say funny things at 11:30 P.M. five nights a week, fifty-two weeks a year. Okay, you can throw in a guest friend or enemy on Monday nights. There are, for our writers, as well as for most decent people, "slow news days" when the newspapers and the supermarket tabloids don't print enough interesting articles to inspire hilarious jokes and a confident feeling that "it will be hilarious if Johnny says . . ."

You can imagine how delighted our writer fellows were, on such a day, when a subject (i.e., my diary) emerged that could lead to put-down humor, particularly if the target area (i.e., me) was someone who had, for the past few days, been highly critical of their comedic attempts.

The diary, and the number of years I have been keeping it, led Ray and Kevin and Hal and Larry and Bob and Mike and Jim and Darrell and Andrew (I did mention that there is a sizable group of highly paid people who are in charge of Johnny's ad libs) to create a new comedy spot for the show called "Excerpts from Fred's Diaries." They wrote it, our audiences laughed at it, Johnny enjoyed doing it, and a new "funny spot" joined "Carnac the Magnificent" and "Aunt Blabby" and "Floyd R. Turbo" and "Art Fern" on the program.

Please picture Johnny at his desk as he explains to the audience:

Excerpts from Fred's Diaries

JOHNNY (SETUP)

Our producer, Fred de Cordova, has had a lengthy show-business career, working with such stars as Jack Benny, George Burns, Errol Flynn, and Ronald Reagan in the movie *Bedtime for Bonzo,* which Fred actually directed. He has also dated some of Hollywood's most glamorous actresses, including Joan Crawford, Ava Gardner, and Lana Turner. It so happens that Fred has kept an extensive diary throughout his career. I am going to share with you selected excerpts from de Cordova's diary.

These are in no particular chronological order. I'll just skip around.

June 15, 1932:
Today I graduated from Harvard Law School. This training will come in handy for my life's goal—pointing at a Nebraska Protestant for a commercial break.

October 2, 1945:
The Chicago Cubs won the pennant today. They are a great team and should do it again real soon.

October 26, 1925:
Read an interesting item in the paper today. A three-day-old baby named Johnny Carson couldn't make his baptism and had David Letterman fill in for him.

October 29, 1929:
The blackest day in history—the stock market crashed and at Chasen's the swordfish was served to me overdone.

July 12, 1963:
Things are going well. Today I was made the director of *The Jack Benny Show.* Soon I'll be able to quit my night job—selling papier-mâché elephants car to car at the Tijuana border.

November 8, 1966:
I had to fire my gardener because he sat around singing all day. I told him, "You'll never work again, Julio Iglesias."

May 8, 1943:
I had a date with the Andrews sisters tonight. I received a good-night kiss, got stood up, and scored.

Dear Diary:
Today I'm up in northern California on vacation, driving through the giant redwoods I planted as a boy.

April 2, 1983:
Hitler's Diary came out today. I can't believe he dated Joan Crawford too.

October 2, 1962:
Today I had my first meeting with Ed McMahon. He greeted me with a hearty laugh and a handshake. Then

he stripped to his shorts and dove into a vat of margaritas.

Dear Diary:
One of my inventor friends came up with a really great idea today—fire.

Dear Diary:
At lunch I went to the commissary with the second in command, Peter Lassally. I wish he'd stop holding that pocket mirror up to my mouth.

This entry is from last Tuesday . . .
Dear Diary:
NBC tried to retire me, claiming my memory was starting to go. I threatened to quit *The Tonight Show* and take Jack Paar with me.

Dear Diary:
Lost my temper today. Told Doc he didn't know how to play the trumpet. Told Ed he was a lousy announcer. Told Johnny he was a genius.

December 9, 1963:
Went to Johnny's wedding. I told him, "The second time's the charm."

March 26, 1977:
I came down hard on Johnny today. I told him if he didn't do things my way, that's perfectly all right with me.

July 5, 1972:
Johnny asked me if he should marry again. I told him, "What have you got to lose?"

February 6, 1984:
Well, I did it. I walked right into Johnny's office and demanded a raise. It will be good practice for when Johnny comes back from vacation.

Dear Diary:
Here's something I never told anyone: I think Jack Benny said "Well" better than President Reagan.

July 8, 1976:
Johnny was on my back again today. Still, it's good exercise carrying the guy around.

Here's a page that's blank. . . . Oh, it says, "Keeping this page open for when I get invited to Johnny's next wedding."

I hope you recognized that many of the items mentioned are entirely fictitious. I rarely, for instance, dated *all* the Andrews sisters.

So the audience laughed, Johnny found it fun to do, and that was the end of that. Right? Wrong! It so happened that super literary agent Irving Lazar watches *The Tonight Show* on a regular basis. Instead of being an amused viewer and phoning me the next day to rib me about some of the jokes, he decided that my actual diaries could serve as a valuable basis for a book about the fascinating life I had led—and was leading until I agreed to write about it.

He talked to me and I listened and I laughed at the notion. He continued to talk and I continued to listen and laugh. Finally money came into the conversation and I stopped laughing. So here it is.

But remember what I told you: if you don't enjoy what you are about to read, it's not my fault. Keep in mind all those *Tonight Show* writers and never forget about Irving Lazar.

PART ONE

Welcome to The Tonight Show

For the past seventeen years most of the entries in my diary have referred to events and personalities involved with the "T.S." and with "J.C." and, on occasion, with several Mrs. J.C.s. During that time span (1970–87) my major focus has been on maintaining the quality and successful track record of the late-night talk-variety television program. In order to do that, it has been necessary to spend a great amount of time with, and around, one of the most fascinating and complex entertainment figures in the entire history of television. I have managed to sneak in some other activities and relationships that we'll discuss in these pages, but for now let's zero in on "T.S."—*The Tonight Show*—and "J.C."—its shining star, Johnny Carson.

11:30 P.M. on the NBC Network

The Tonight Show Starring Johnny Carson is a phenomenon. It is almost impossible to think of anyone you've wanted to see or hear or chat with who hasn't

On one of six happy evenings. Emmys make nice decorations.

been a guest on the show. Also, it's possible that there have been more than a few you could easily have done without. But you can eliminate any of them in mid-sentence simply by pushing a button. Don't you wish you could do that with some of your dinner guests?

Think about it. Just about everyone from Tiny Tim to Bill Buckley, from Arnold Palmer to Carl Sagan, from Frank Sinatra to George Burns (my two favorite singers) has walked through that multicolored curtain to be greeted courteously by Nebraska's best-known product.

Johnny Carson didn't invent *The Tonight Show*. A very bright NBC executive did. And Johnny wasn't the first host. He was preceded by Jerry Lester, Steve Allen, and Jack Paar, and each of them contributed his special talents to late-night entertainment. But for the past twenty-five years there has been, night after night (except for a guest host every now and then), one man, and one man only, who has functioned as the King of Midnight. My Boss. I refer to him in that fashion because what he says is what we do—and also because there's a clause in my contract that stipulates the use of that term at least once a day.

The opposing networks—ABC and CBS, if you are alphabet-oriented—have tried everything they could think of to shake Johnny from the number-one spot. But nothing has worked. Merv Griffin, Joey Bishop, Dick Cavett, Jerry Lewis, Sammy Davis, Jr., Allan Thicke (Jack Paar even made an ill advised comeback effort), and the latest entry, Joan Rivers (and more about that lady later), have taken Johnny on head to head. All of them fired and fell back. Reruns of prime-time programs: *Kojak, Rockford Files, Magnum, P.I., Hawaii Five-O;* original programming such as *Mary Hartman, Mary Hartman, Honeymoon Hotel*—that didn't work, either. ABC even changed its format and installed a first-class journalist, Ted Koppel, in the

5

11:30 spot, feeling that the public might enjoy viewing the problems of the day—one more time—before turning out the lights. Only on election nights, or during hostage situations, or famous last words, may there be a for-one-night viewer swing; but nearly every morning when I am given the Nielsen ratings, there it is: *The Tonight Show* was watched by more people than viewed the other two networks combined.

And why, you are entitled to ask, is this the case? After all, the guests on *The Tonight Show* are, in spite of all my efforts, essentially the same people you see on the other chat shows. And you are smart enough to realize that they are in attendance because they have something to plug—a new book that will soon appear in your nearby bookstore, an album that is about to be released, an upcoming movie in which they have a percentage deal, or a video cassette that will explain how you can lose thirty pounds in thirty days. We all know that these important folks don't show up because they need the $490 they'll be paid, minus the usual withholdings.

No, the movie and television stars and the recording giants make themselves available to serve their own purposes—and there's nothing wrong with that. But we are discussing why, inasmuch as they pop up all over your radio dial and your television programs, so many more people choose to watch them on *The Tonight Show*. It is my personal opinion—and NBC appears to support my position to the extent of paying him (I'll get more specific later) a bundle—that, no matter who the guests are, viewers tune in because the host of the show is Johnny Carson.

Who says that he's the reason? And if it's true, why is he the reason? I suggest that you keep turning the pages.

Johnny's "welcome" to me when I joined the show. Perry, Art, Stan and Rudy were my predecessors as producers of the program.

President Ford, Bill Demarest and I—three rather danger-ous golfers.

On the Tour

I play a lot of golf. Mostly I play at my home course—Bel Air—which is a fifteen-minute drive from my home. I have my regular group of friends and enemies and we all look forward to playing with, and against, each other. Bel Air has among its members some of the most famous motion-picture, television, sports, and recording stars extant. I'll drop a few names: Dean Martin, Bob Newhart, Mac Davis, Andy Williams, Fred MacMurray, Pat Boone, Jim Garner, Johnny Carson, Robert Goulet, Dick Martin, Tom Harmon, Joe Namath, Bob Stack, Richard Crenna, Jimmy Stewart, Glen Campbell, Vic Damone, Mike Douglas, and Peter Ueberroth.

It will come as no surprise to you that all of these folks live in attractive and well-run homes, and only when jobs and work assignments or domestic upheavals require them to leave town do they do so, and then with considerable reluctance. But there is another call to duty that all of these "names" and lesser lights, such as I, find it hard to refuse. We pack our bags, explain to our wives that we'll be back in a few days, forgo our freshly squeezed orange juice, and spend a considerable amount of our own money. The reason? It's called the Celebrity Golf Tour.

About thirty weekends a year, maybe more, a very worthwhile charity sponsors a golf tournament in its hometown—Menomonee Falls, Wisconsin; El Paso, Texas; Hilton Head, South Carolina; Charleston, West Virginia; Tampa, Florida, for instance. To aid in raising large sums of money, well-known people leave their lares and penates and fly, coach, to the area designated. Local business men and women and social leaders pay as much as three thousand dollars per person to be golf partners of celebrities. The proceeds (and they can be surprisingly large) benefit the sponsoring charity. The celebrity usually plays two rounds of golf and attends cocktail parties and rubber-chicken dinners, stays up too late, and tees off too early the next morning.

I play in about fifteen of these events every year. Given the comforts of my home and the nonending schedule of *The Tonight Show,* why do I do it? Certainly it isn't because I'm a do-gooder at heart. Primarily it's because these trips get me away from the inbred Hollywood Syndrome, with its slightly warped point of view, and more closely involved with the men and women who comprise the audience of our show.

The people I meet on the tour seem to know me in a second-hand fashion as "that fellow Johnny keeps talking to during the show." They sense that I'm a friend of his, and that, in turn, makes me a friend of theirs. They regularly ask me to give him their regards. Over and over I am told that they have been watching him "for twenty years" or "ever since we started looking at TV" and they invariably stress how much he means to them. Many of the younger group tell me that their parents are his fans, they are his fans, and on Friday nights they allow their children to stay up and watch the show. Three generations of America is pretty impressive.

Several times over the years, it's been reported in the newspapers that contract negotiations between NBC and Carson have bogged down and that Johnny might decide he's been at it long enough. On these occasions, his fans invariably seek me out and tell me they'd appreciate it if I would urge Johnny to give in a little on his network demands because they have been "going to bed with him" for years and it's truly important to them that he stay on the air. They don't give a damn about the economics involved—whether NBC or their favorite guy is in the right; they just want him to show up where he's always been at 11:30 every night of their lives.

Because they watch the show regularly they are aware that during the taping I sit about twelve feet from Johnny, directly in front of him and squarely in his eye line, and that I function as a sounding board when the going gets rough. Sometimes they extend their interest in Johnny to include such questions as: "Just what is it you do on the show?" Prepared as I am to discuss, in some detail, the many values I bring to the finished product, it becomes quickly evident that a little knowledge of my activities is sufficient. They really want to know what I know about the Man himself—his personal characteristics, his private life, and his plans. Let's start with the plans.

For years the press has indicated that Johnny may be ready to pack it in. After all, how much longer can he want to continue doing the same thing? And how much longer can the network give in to his "absurd" demands? And surely there are many other things he'd like to do. Let's be honest. If Johnny decided he had hosted *The Tonight Show* long enough, if he opted to walk away from the every-night pressure, or if he chose to enjoy himself doing specials and variety shows or playing live concerts around the country for a couple of hundred thousand dollars a night, who could blame him? He's worked hard enough and long enough—he's entitled. I'd lose a bundle every week if my salary stopped coming in, but that's not Johnny's problem; it's my wife's.

But, for sure, it would upset all these folks I've been telling you about, the folks I meet on the tour. And millions of other people like them. Let's take a few minutes to talk about just what kind of person can engender a following of fifteen or twenty million people who constitute a cross section of our population and who have little in common. What's he like? Apparently it depends on where the information and the character analysis spring from.

If you choose to base your evaluation of Johnny Carson on what you've read in those "accurate" supermarket best-sellers whose basic thrust is to defame and disparage, you might believe that Johnny Carson is in his mid-sixties, an acknowledged loner who has pressured NBC into making him one of the richest figures in the world of entertainment. In spite of his engaging personality while appearing on television, he is almost completely without friends, except for a nonending stream of nubile starlets on whom he lavishes diamonds and furs, while refusing to help his many wives and children make ends meet.

You might also be informed that he lives reclusively in a one-bedroom palace, recently purchased for more than nine million dollars, high atop a bluff overlooking the Pacific Ocean, rarely sees anyone except his Girl of the Month, and reluctantly is driven to work, arriving at NBC barely in time to walk onstage for his television show. Or that he owns not one but two spectacular beach homes, plus the former Mervyn LeRoy home in Bel Air, a condo on fashionable Wilshire Boulevard, and, when he ventures East, a beautifully furnished apartment in the Pierre Hotel, as well as a triplex in the fabulous Trump Tower.

And you might have read about his always-standing-by nine-passenger jet plane, his fleet of luxury automobiles (his DeLorean would certainly be mentioned), his Johnny Carson Apparel Company, his network of television stations, his investments in cattle and oil, and his personally owned bank.

The above would likely be highlighted by carefully chosen photographs, slightly out of focus, showing him scowling at autograph seekers and surrounded by various scantily clothed actresses.

And there would be a summation paragraph headlined: THE SAD LIFE OF A MAN WHO COULD HAVE HAD IT ALL.

With apologies to a Mr. Cosell, why don't I tell it like it is?

Johnny Carson is a thoroughly decent and considerate man. His Iowa–Nebraska upbringing has taught him the value of a dollar, but he is enormously charitable. As is true of Frank Sinatra, his financial aid to many less fortunate friends and acquaintances is severely underpublicized, at his request. He is unfailingly polite to strangers, even when they brashly intrude on his privacy, often in restaurants but on occasion in men's rooms. He is completely aware of his star status but never throws his weight around. He is extremely intolerant of stupidity and carelessness in those who work for him, and is also harshly critical of the mistakes he himself makes. He has been a fine son and a fine father, but the jury is still out on his status as a husband. There might be several dissenting opinions. But I have a hunch—a very strong one—that his most recent venture into the Land of Matrimony will be a happy and permanent one. He and Alex have fun together.

He is sixty-one years old, in excellent physical condition (he works out at least three days a week in a private gym), and plays a better-than-average (celebrity-type) tennis game. He has indeed recently purchased an extremely expensive ocean-view home (for considerably less than the published price, however) and loves it and its views—which have been described as featuring Mexico to the south, Japan directly ahead, and Alaska to the north. To tuck in a personal opinion, it is a gorgeous home.

When he bought the house, it had only one bedroom (the choice of the builder), but now revisions have made it less of a showplace and more of a home. The living room is, to be truthful, so vast that when he first saw it, a friend asked, "Where's the gift shop?" Sure it's a sensational place, and at an atypical "open house," everyone agreed on one thing: no matter what it cost, it's worth it, and they all wished they could afford one like it.

Now let's take a page or two to rebut some of these comments about Johnny's life-style:

1. He sold the "other" beach house to John McEnroe, the proceeds from which represented a sizable portion of his payment for the new house.

2. The beautiful home in Bel Air was once the family dwelling place of the Carsons but now is the West Coast residence of Mrs. *Joanna* Carson. You may have read that they aren't living together these days—and nights. Divorce and remarriage will change things like that.

3. The condo on Wilshire Boulevard serves as an alternate address for Johnny when business (or pleasure) dictates that he stay in town.

4. The Pierre Hotel apartment in New York is the divorce-decreed Eastern headquarters of Mrs. Joanna Carson and has not been visited by Mr. Carson since the domestic to-do—even though J.C. would love to regain some of the personal possessions that still re-

main unavailable to him since the locks were suddenly changed.

5. Trump Tower's triplex is actually a duplex—and is for sale. Judging from some of the recent offers, it will likely turn out to be another of Johnny's whimsical purchases that invariably turn a tidy profit.

6. "His" jet is a corporate plane—sometimes used by him but much more often leased out to outside companies and other individuals. And while an expensive luxury, it will probably wind up as a break-even item.

7. There is no chauffeur on his payroll, nor is he limo-oriented, he drives himself to work, to restaurants, and to social functions in a very nice Chevy Corvette. He recently bought a Ford Bronco and he has a vintage Mercedes, which was his main car till the Corvette replaced it. Yes, there was a DeLorean —a symbol of a not-too-successful investment.

8. Sure he's made investments—some good, some bad. His "network" of TV stations is a part ownership in one, he did buy a bank (and wishes he hadn't), and he's enormously proud of the success of his Johnny Carson Apparel Company.

So what's the big deal? He earned his riches, he pays his taxes, and his only shortcoming, apparently, is his continued success.

Far from the image the tabloid journals paint, the Carson picture is a very respectable one.

Johnny is an extremely private person and admits it. He believes that what he does when he is off camera is his own business. He is not a volunteerer of where he went last night, who was there and what they did. He does not gossip and isn't interested in hearing it. He goes to dinner parties on occasion, but in most instances he would rather not; he feels that his conversations with his guests "on the air" are all the small talk he needs for that day. Ken Tynan, in a

Carson profile for *The New Yorker* of February 20, 1978, wrote that Johnny would be a more outgoing guest at a party if the other guests had red lights on their foreheads—as do television cameras.

The Carson circle of close friends is a small one and that's by his choice. His prominence in the world of entertainment and the format of *The Tonight Show* insure a vast number of acquaintances—to whom he is unfailingly polite. He's primarily a listener, and his sense of humor is as strong and as quick offstage as it is on. But, given his choice, he would much rather go directly home after the show, read, watch television, and retire early.

Johnny's closest male companion is, by far, his lawyer and advisor, Henry Bushkin. It is usually with Henry that Johnny has a quiet dinner at Morton's or Spago. If a small group is invited to Johnny's home over a weekend, Henry will be there; in the occasional Carson poker games (one a medium-stakes game) the participants regularly include Steve Martin, Chevy Chase, producer Dan Melnick, and Henry Bushkin. In a small-stakes game the players include Bobby Quinn (the show's director), Bud Robinson (Doc Severinsen's manager), Jim Mahoney (Carson Company's publicist), me—and Henry Bushkin. When, in my *Tonight Show* position, I find it necessary to make an important decision, I, of course, check it out with Johnny. He will invariably tell me to check it out with Henry. After Henry, Johnny is closest with Bobby Quinn, and my seventeen years of tenure indicates an acceptance of me as a friend. You can see by now that the "close circle" has a direct correlation to *The Tonight Show*.

Don't misunderstand—there are many "names" and "not names" with whom Johnny has fun, to whose homes he goes and looks forward to going. The next day at the office he's liable to mention that he had a good time at the Lew Wassermans' (Lew is the top man at Universal and probably in the entire industry) or at the Lazars' or at the Billy Wilders'. A good time for Carson requires a simple menu, intelligent conversation, and an early departure.

There are three Carson sons—Chris, Rick, and Cory. All are grown by now, and the father-son relationship is a close one. Not on a day-by-day basis, but if there is any kind of crisis, you can count on the boys to be in evidence. If they have a problem, Johnny is there. Add to the close group his brother, Dick, and his sister, Catherine.

Johnny was at one time a pretty good drinker. Strike that, he was a pretty bad drinker. He didn't drink a lot, but he didn't have to—in the middle of his third martini you were aware of a change in the weather. So was he. Now he is just this side of a teetotaler—every now and then a glass or two of wine; more often, Perrier.

Mr. Carson does have a temper. It's been directed at me a few times. Almost without exception his anger relates to some real or fancied dereliction of duty by *The Tonight Show* staff. He demands the same amount of dedication to the program as he has and can't abide a mistake caused by lack of attention to all details. A mechanical or technical error is understandable and semi-acceptable, but human mistakes are beyond the pale. Once the storm has subsided and a presumably intelligent explanation of "what really happened" has been made, he is gracious, sorry he blew his cool, but not at all sure the explanation was a valid one.

It is likely that the same quickness to anger and the rapid return to calm exists on the domestic front at his home. I can't be really sure, because I don't spend a great deal of time there.

Unlike the case with a large number of other stars, there seems to be no jealousy in Johnny's makeup. He is the first to praise the programs and performances of others, even if on occasion they are in a time slot opposite his. He is much less generous with himself and is also the first to point out how much better or funnier he could have been.

You may have noticed that I've skirted the "all-those-marriages" syndrome. I never met his first wife, Jody, but I've never heard him make a disparaging remark about her. Wife number two, Joanne, played a major part in my winding up with Johnny. Maybe "major" is a little strong. At a social gathering one night long ago she mentioned to Johnny that I'd be a good producer for him if he decided to make a change. Her suggestion had something less than immediate impact: eleven months later he took her advice.

The most recent ex-Mrs. Carson, Joanna (with a final "a"), was, until her divorce, a very good friend of the de Cordovas. My wife and I were, in fact, having dinner with Johnny at "21" in New York when he first caught a glimpse of her across that crowded room. He moved quickly, learned her name, obtained her phone number, and the future was clear. Maybe not. During their courtship, I asked him if marriage to Joanna was on the horizon. Johnny gave me the piercing look you've seen so often on television and said, "Fred, if ever you think I am getting close to another marriage, you have my permission to punch me—as hard as you can—on the point of my jaw." I didn't punch him, he got married, and during the happy days of their marriage, Janet and I spent a good deal of social time with Joanna and Johnny. We were truly sorry that their relationship broke apart. But his recent marriage to Alexis Mass came as no surprise to me. Johnny had constantly indicated his happiness with their relationship and regularly talked of their similar tastes and reactions and evaluations. In the past Johnny has always paid for his thrills—I feel those days are over.

I am, however, no authority on why some marriages work and others don't—I have been married only once: to Janet, for almost twenty-four years.

Summation of the man: Johnny is a major star and thoroughly aware of the problems and pleasures that go with that territory. *The Tonight Show* is enormously important to him, and I feel that he'll be extremely unhappy if and when he decides he's had enough. He is, as I hope I've made clear, a private but not hostile man with as many close friends as he wants, all devoted to him. He's rich and lives well, but has his first show-business contract—a twelve-dollar "gig"—framed in his den so he'll never forget the early days. He's fun to be with, and I promise you there isn't a phony bone in his body.

Behind
The Tonight Show
Curtain

We have now established that Johnny is a real good guy, that he's been a star for a long time, and that he's bright and funny. I guess that just about sums up why *The Tonight Show* is such a big success. Actually there's a little bit more to it than that—a little more that has been kept secret until now. Let me explain.

There seems to be nothing more exciting to the average, or above-average, American than an unauthorized peek behind the scenes. Thrill number one is to sneak past the No Visitors Allowed sign.

In attempting to pander to this phenomenon, the world of entertainment has created the legend that publicity is one of the major bases of success. Columnists, fan magazines, trade journals, advertisements, and talk shows spew forth every minute detail—true or untrue—about the private lives of celebrities. We are told who sleeps with whom, who is pregnant without benefit of marriage, who has homosexual tendencies, who is in financial trouble, who had an operation on what private part, who is "into" booze or dope, and who has given how much to what charity . . . and is furious that the news has found its way into the media.

The chagrin that regularly results from these disclosures is difficult to "buy" when we realize that individuals, networks, motion-picture studios, record companies, and publishers all employ, and pay sizable sums to, publicity firms and press agents whose sole purpose is to make sure that even the most trivial activities of their clients make their way into print. Even some of the most reclusive of public figures pay representatives to issue releases stressing how much the recluse dislikes publicity. Greta Garbo, as you probably know, denies that she ever said "I vant to be alone." But someone said she did.

How, you ask, does this involve *The Tonight Show?* You've been spoon-fed reams of publicity about Johnny Carson. You are certainly aware that Ed McMahon is able to outdrink a thirsty Clydesdale, has been known to laugh heartily at a feeble joke, and is happy to announce that "you may already have won a million dollars." You have been informed that Doc Severinsen is considered one of the world's top trumpet players, owns racehorses that invariably chase other horses, and dresses strangely—but only to amuse Johnny and our audiences. You may even be aware that the Prince of Polyester, Tommy Newsom, replaces Doc as our conductor when Doc replaces Ed as our announcer when a guest host replaces Johnny "behind the desk."

But, if you ponder it for a moment, that's just about all you know about *The Tonight Show*. How our show is put together—how the guests are chosen, who selects the guest hosts, why it is that some performers appear so often and some never appear at all, who are the people who compose the staff, and a score of other "inside" details has never been publicized. And that's not by accident.

I doubt that a day passes without a request from a respected (and some not so) magazine, columnist, or newspaper asking for a story on the day-by-day, behind-the-scenes activities of our program. I always explain that such stories are off limits, and, as a result, there is the assumption that there must be dreadful secrets that are being carefully hidden from the public. Of course there are secrets, but they aren't even slightly dreadful.

Johnny and I have always felt, since the start of our association, that what happens during the preparation of our show is our business and ours alone. We believe that what appears on the air is what counts—not the aches and pains we suffer before the final product is packaged and presented on the tube. Of course we face minor or major problems every day, but we're all paid handsomely to make sure the seams don't show.

However, since I enforce the rule, who better to break it? So let's lift the curtain of silence and tell the complete story of *The Tonight Show*. Let's name the people involved, the chain of command, tell how decisions are made and who makes them, why some people rarely appear on the show and others appear too often, let's name a few names, uncover some of the mistakes we've made, see who takes the blame— and let's hope you find it all as exciting and dicey as we do.

Who is "we"? If you eliminate the stage crew, the technicians, the publicity personnel assigned to us by NBC, the lawyers and accountants and business-affairs "helpers," you'll be surprised at the very small number of people who actually put the show together. For good or bad, there's been very little turnover in that group. Both Johnny and the staff are very loyal to the show, and with very few exceptions, we've stuck together through a great deal of thick and a smattering of thin. Marriages, illness, and sheer stupidity have caused only a few departures from our frenzied circle.

We are all aware that we have considerable responsibility in organizing and telecasting a brand-new hour-long program five nights a week. There is no out-of-town tryout during which wrinkles can be ironed out, we can't come back the next day for rewrites or retakes, and we can't edit and patch the show after it's been done. What you see on the tube is what we did. I think that's what makes it so much fun for Johnny, for us, and, hopefully, for you.

Who, you still ask? Okay, let's start at the top. There's just one boss—and don't you forget it. He is involved in every facet of every show and wants it that way. He'd rather not be bothered by details that we should be able to handle by ourselves, but if we find ourselves in a bind, he's prepared to listen to background, decide on a course of action, and take the blame if he makes the wrong decision. Ordinarily he makes the right one. Later, if we should have been able to work things out without bothering him, he's liable to point that out. He's impatient with inefficiency and deeply concerned with the quality of every show. He's also quick to blame himself if he feels he could have conducted a better interview or performed a comedy sketch more cleverly. He prefers, I've learned over the years, to make that evaluation himself.

As executive producer, I am number two on the firing line. I am totally responsible to the public and to Johnny for who and what appears on the show. That means it is my ultimate decision to choose the guests, oversee the subject matter of the interviews, approve the song selections and their length, determine the amount of time allotted to each guest, the order in which the performers should appear, when we should break away for a commercial, and whether a guest should be "bumped" and rescheduled . . . and I read and report to J.C. my evaluation of the sketches and desk spots. The monologue alone is out of my jurisdiction—only his monologue writers have a hint of that until the show is on the air. In general, I'm to blame if anything goes wrong; if all goes well, and it usually does, there's little back-slapping—we just move on to tomorrow's problems.

Lest I sound a bit manic, there are several experienced and talented folks who have considerable input. These aren't the "little people" you hear about in acceptance speeches; these are professionals who could easily move in and take over if, God forbid, I tarried too long on the golf course or took up residence at Forest Lawn.

And the first of these is my truly valued colleague and advisor, Peter Lassally. For many years he was my associate producer and now holds the title of producer. When my predecessor, Rudy Tellez, left the staff, Peter was first in line to replace him. Out of the blue I was offered the job, was delighted to accept, moved to New York City, and wound up as Rudy's replacement. Peter was from the start most gracious to me, helped me constantly as I learned my chores, and never indicated his disappointment. For seventeen years he has been my trusted right arm, has stepped in for me in my absences, and I can't imagine a closer and warmer relationship than ours. Peter was for many years the producer of the Arthur Godfrey Show, he knows everyone in our business, he is a nonstop television watcher, a foe of bad taste (no matter how popular it may be), and I recognize how frustrating it must be for him that I remain healthy and in attendance. His devoted wife, Alice, must have grown weary sticking pins in her Freddie doll.

Bobby Quinn is our director and has been for over

twenty years. He worked on *The Tonight Show* as an assistant director and before that as a stage manager, as far back as the Jack Paar era. He moved into the director's chair when Dick Carson (Johnny's brother) left that job for greener pastures. Dick was the longtime director of *The Merv Griffin Show* and still handles *Wheel of Fortune*—both very successful operations. Dick and Johnny remain close friends and see each other often. They share the same laid-back charm and sense of humor and could easily be mistaken one for the other. But back to Quinny.

Of all of us, I think Carson and Quinn are the most joined at the hip. They were drinking pals back in the days when Johnny drank and a couple of the Mrs. Carsons felt that Bobby was, during that period, something less than a good influence on their husband. They think and react alike, and if you tangle with Bobby, you tangle with Johnny. It is one of my major regrets that the viewing public—and the Emmy Awards structure—fail to recognize what a major contributor Bobby Quinn has been to the success of *The Tonight Show*. Just try to think of the last time you wanted to see Johnny's reaction to some comment and the camera wasn't there. I can't, either.

Now you are about to meet the breed apart—the coordinators. That's a made-up title for five individuals who are the bloodstream of the program. They are remarkable and have to be. Possibly you'll understand what they do if I call them writer/booker/researchers. One of their job functions is to discover new guests for the program, and that's not easy. But it isn't their most difficult assignment; they must also find new areas of conversation for guests who are appearing on our show for the umpteenth time. They must keep our audiences from feeling they've heard all this before—talk-show déjà vu. They are required to view an endless supply of video cassettes sent to us by agents, friends, cuckoos, parents, and the general public—all of whom are sure that their "discovery" will be a major find. Every now and then they come across a nugget, but mostly they don't and a courteous letter of rejection must be sent back with the cassette. They read and view everything that might lead to a new, or revitalized, appearance on the show. They are highly paid and deserve to be. And *The Tonight Show* has caused all of them to be a little strange.

Each coordinator lives or dies, so to speak, depending on the success or failure of his assigned guest on the show. Whoever the guest is, he or she is, for that night, the coord's baby. Whether he admires or loathes the person assigned to him, for the ten or fifteen minutes that his charge is sitting next to Johnny, the coord is on the hot spot. Is the audience attentive? Is Johnny bored? Is the anecdote that seemed so amusing earlier still so on the air? The mood of each coord depends completely on how his guest "came off." They care. I told you they were strange. The coords are, in order of seniority:

Shirley Wood. She's no longer the youngest girl in town, but she's still one of the most attractive. Shirley has been with the Carson Show since its inception, and there isn't a recognizable person on the face of the earth she hasn't dated, interviewed, coddled, or coerced. Single by choice, she could have married any of a number of our guests who have been bedazzled by her. She has "hot-bathed" Robert Blake in order to overcome his backaches and get him to the show on time, she has nursed Peter O'Toole carefully through the cocktail hour and delivered him, almost coherent, to the entrance curtain, and she has calmed the fears and concerns of empty-headed starlets who could barely, without her help, get from the ladies' room to the panel. She is one of a kind. The most cynical lady I've ever met and, at the same time, a certified marshmallow.

Bob Dolce. He is a New Yorker by birth but a dedicated Italian by emotion. He has established himself as the foremost authority in the world of the theater. Everyone knows the stars; Bob knows the history and the life-style of every featured and bit player. He doesn't care how good their performance onstage may be; he knows whether or not there is ten minutes of talk-show "amuse" in their background. He has endeared himself to such "easy-to-get-along-with" personalities as Shelley Winters, Cybill Shepherd, Peggy Lee, Susan Sarandon, Peter Strauss, Richard Benjamin, and Tony Bennett and still loves the world of show business—and some of the people who inhabit it.

Jim McCawley. He's a pixie and can't seem to do anything about it. He has, often, given up drinking, but drinking doesn't seem to be the problem. His dedication to his job has made a shambles of his marriage. I'm completely in sympathy with his wife. He is, you see, the man who discovers all the brand-new comedians who continually appear on our program. He is our "comedy maven," and to maintain that position, it is necessary for him to catch the performances of comedians when they appear at the Comedy Store, the Improv, and all the other night clubs—obscure or well known—where they have the opportunity to display their talents. He is at the office all day and on the town all night and has often slept on his office couch in order to be on time for the morning meeting. He is primarily responsible for the discovery of, and the selection of the material for, the long list of young comedians our show is so proud of. His wife often phones me to inquire about his health—and whereabouts.

Jim has recently been elevated to the position of associate producer of *The Tonight Show*. He now shares with Peter and me many of the procedural duties of a decision maker, plus all his former activities, and as a result, he has even less time to devote to his home life. His new title and responsibilities require him to attend the after-show "post mortem" in Mr. Carson's office (Peter, Quinn, and I are the remaining mourners), and he is, therefore, privy to any and all comments about the ups and downs of that evening's events. On occasion that can spark the need for a quick vodka on the rocks before facing the rest of the world and its petty problems.

Debbie Vickers. Our fourth coord is the youngest and has been with us for only three years. During her tryout period we were afraid that she might be too polite and trusting for the job—possibly too inclined to see the *good* in people. But her ability to dig beneath the surface and to recognize talent was quickly apparent. Exposure to the rest of us quickly removed any vestiges of her belief in the integrity and honesty of the agents and publicity representatives she was assigned to deal with, and today she is unlikely to believe anything she is told. And we're all rather proud of what we have done to her.

Darcy Hettrich has recently joined us and has been assigned to the highest risk area—the search for "civilians." Darcy's job is to uncover non-show-biz folks who may be amusing to our audience because they (a) have the longest mustache in the world, (b) are the oldest man to parachute from a plane, (c) own a dog that will climb a tree, or (d) are the shortest man in the Marine Corps. Her office is filled with video cassettes, clippings, and letters heralding the activities of "the oldest," "the youngest," "the shortest," and the "most absurd" people in the world.

All she has to do is interview them, find out if they

can talk and see and hear and travel, separate the "cuties" from the "crazies," evaluate their on-air personalities, convince me they should be booked, and then sit in a state of frozen fear while they chat with Johnny on the show. These civilians are far and away Johnny's favorite part of the show, and he is at his best when he deals with them.

So you can see that a number of people contribute to the program. But there is a creative group for whom I have a special regard. Theirs is the most difficult job of all. Most of us have, on occasion, said something funny and we've been delighted when people laughed. But how would you like to make a living making people laugh?

Our writing staff faces that problem every day.

The Writers

The Lord created Heaven and Earth and, as an immediate afterthought, writers. Smart as He was, He knew that He couldn't think of everything by Himself. We all have been told that "first came the Word," and it was necessary for someone to write it. The Word is written to make people cry and to make people laugh and to make people contribute to worthy causes. Our writing staff is asked to concentrate on the laughter area and to count on Johnny to contribute. As a stimulus they are very highly paid—and they earn every penny. Johnny, who at one time was a comedy writer for Red Skelton, is most empathetic to the problems of his writing staff. He is aware that a novelist can take years to complete a novel, that a screenplay can take months to create and polish, and that his writers must service him every day. He is also aware that what they write he must perform—and sometimes he's not quite as sympathetic as I've indicated above.

Our writing "guys" or "boys"—always alluded to in those terms no matter how old and decrepit they may be—are divided into two groups. The monologue writers arrive at 9:00 A.M. and live in a world of their own. World War III breaks out, their homes catch on fire, their bagels don't get toasted—too bad. They just write their jokes and go home. Hal Goodman, Larry Klein, Mike Barrie, Jim Mulholland, and Bob Keane operate without any supervision other than Johnny's. By ten o'clock they have read the front pages, the sports pages, the society pages, checked the magazine covers and the headlines of the "scandal sheets," and decided what current event lends itself to a comedic twist, and each of them writes, and submits, twenty or thirty jokes to J.C. From this batch of pages, Carson chooses those he thinks most effective, adds some pertinent observations—and the first ten minutes of our show are accounted for.

Group two handles the "material" area. They supply the next ten minutes of the program. Ray Siller, Kevin Mulholland, Darrell Vickers, and Andrew Nicholls—working as a group—are currently involved. (Many others have come and gone.) It is their task to write "The Mighty Carson Art Players" sketches, "Carnac the Magnificent," the editorial rebuttals of "Floyd R. Turbo," "Aunt Blabby," the sales pitches of Art Fern (your "Tea Time Movie" salesman of shoddy merchandise), and, from time to time, "Fred's Diary" entries plus the numerous "desk pieces" featuring Ed McMahon's "surprise" as Johnny recites some hitherto unknown information "which has just come to my attention." The writers do a remarkable job, and Johnny does a remarkable job with what they do.

You may have noticed that I've barely mentioned two of the most visible and valuable contributors to the success of our program. They deserve a few pages devoted entirely to themselves.

Doc was in the band (Skitch Henderson was the leader) when Johnny took over the show. Skitch moved on and Doc moved up front and has been there ever since.

Ed was Johnny's sidekick when he hosted (the grammatically incorrectly named) *Who Do You Trust?* When NBC chose Carson to be *The Tonight Show*'s head man, he brought Ed along with him.

Johnny and Ed and Doc are the "A-Team" and it's a potent trio. Ed appears often on other programs, but never in a competing time slot. He is the spokesperson for a large group of brewers, banks, and insurance companies, and he continues to show up in your mailbox offering to give you that elusive million dollars. But he is always on *The Tonight Show* when Johnny is the host. He has missed a few performances in his twenty-four-plus years because of illness, but the doctors had to strap him down to keep him from showing up.

Doc has more requests to play Las Vegas and the Lake Tahoe resorts and Atlantic City than he can possibly handle. Recently he's become the guest conductor of several symphony orchestras and he's developed a small jazz group, Xebron, which features considerably more far-out music than you hear on our program. He's in demand.

Ed's contract stipulates that he be present when Johnny hosts. He's off duty when Johnny is off. Doc's contract stipulates that he must remain available to us to act as announcer and sidekick when we have a guest host. Tommy Newsom (an outstanding musician and arranger) has a contract that stipulates he must be present to act as conductor when Ed is off and Doc is the announcer. Should there be a problem somewhere in that lineup, Shelly Cohen (our assistant to Doc) moves into action. We can platoon our players when it is necessary.

Neither Ed nor Doc has any desire to host the show. And neither has much input in the booking of our

I thought the invitation said "casual."

guests. Every now and then they'll suggest that someone they saw or heard in performance might be an asset to us. But that's as deep as they go. And I think it's a wise position to take: if booking mistakes are made by me and my staff, Ed and Doc are free from guilt, even by association.

Ed checks with me during the day, by phone or by dropping into my office, to ask if there's anything he should know. I tell him if he is to be part of a sketch or a desk piece and if a rehearsal is scheduled, or if it's better that he play it by ear. There's never been anyone more capable of playing it as it lays.

Doc has no reason to check with me until music-rehearsal time. If it appears that we want a band number on the show, I get word to him—he'll have several ready—and the audience will be pleased. Most of the time the at-home viewers hear only a few notes as we come back on the air from a commercial. Bud Robinson, Doc's manager, chooses the unusual clothes he wears on the program, and they've become an amusing facet of his personality. In private, he's a jeans-and-sport-shirt man.

Both Ed and Doc are very happily married. Each was married before and for each the second time around is clearly better than the first. Doc, it so happens, is married to a lovely and talented scriptwriter who was for a long period of time the executive secretary to the executive producer of *The Tonight Show*.

You have now been introduced to the movers and the shakers. It's time to tell you how they move and shake. You are invited to be present as we put the show together; but you'll have to get up early. The festivities start at 9:30 A.M.—sharp. Be on time!

Step by Step—
Till Your Feet Hurt

My workday starts at home at 7:30 A.M.—no matter how amusing Roger Moore or Jack Lemmon was at a party the night before. Step one is the sampling of the morning TV news shows. I check the *Today* show, *Good Morning America,* and the CBS *Morning News* to find out if there have been any newsbreaks that might affect our show and, more importantly, to see if they are featuring any guests who are pushing their most recent accomplishments and aren't overwhelmingly dull. I'm regularly reminded of those wonderful days when news shows dealt with the news and not with celebrity interviews.

Step two brings me to the printed word. I thumb through the local newspapers, *The New York Times,* the *Washington Post,* and the two important trade papers, *The Hollywood Reporter* and *Daily Variety,* paying most attention to the headlines and the entertainment and gossip sections. Another attempt to make sure that no bookable guest will fall through the cracks.

I'm out of the house and into my car by 9:00— stuffed with the news of the day—and on my way to the lovely and legendary Burbank, California. NBC is nestled, not too imposingly, between the combined Columbia–Warners Studio and the Walt Disney headquarters where Goofy Lane and Daffy Duck Boulevard cross Reality Way. I drive through the gates of my home away from home (where, after seventeen years, the traffic guards still ask me for identification), always reminded by the large signs that read All Vehicles Are Subject to Search upon Exit that NBC will go to any lengths to discover a good script. After slowing nine times to overcome some of the tallest speed bumps in the West, I pull into my parking place in front of the impressively named Tonight Show Complex. Less flamboyantly described, television's most lucrative production is housed in a prefab, triple-width, one-story-high trailer. Its lack of style is compensated for, however, by its views of identical monstrosities on either side.

It's now 9:30. Billie Freebairn-Smith, my charming, efficient, and sassy secretary, is at her desk. She smiles warmly and suggests that I may wish to return home immediately rather than face the problems that are neatly described on my desk. Some of the time she is fooling; most of the time she is not. I sit at my desk, glance at the array of video cassettes, phone messages, letters, albums, and books. By that time, Billie enters with some coffee and a list of people I promised to "get back to" first thing in the morning.

About the coffee. It is not demeaning, as the office manuals insist, that Billie brings me a cup in the morning. We have a deal. Once a day I do the same for her, properly creamed and sugared. The fact that she doesn't drink coffee is her problem, not mine.

It is most important that, first of all, I "check the board." Directly behind my desk there is a twenty-four-foot wall, cork-covered and divided into thirty-one vertical segments, one for each day of the month

36

and so numbered. Under each date is the name of the day's host—either Johnny or a substitute (as we speak, Jay Leno); Ed's and Doc's names (unless they are scheduled to be on vacation) are followed by cards bearing the names of the personalities who are booked to appear on that day. Each name is on a separate card —pink if the booking is firm, white with a crayoned "O" if an offer has been made but no positive answer has been received, blue if the hoped-for guest is a minor or a non-citizen (in which case special school or immigration clearances are necessary) and many plain white cards indicating that so-and-so might be a good idea but not *so* good that an offer has been made.

Other symbols on the cards may be:

S . . . song will be performed
SPS . . . booking calls for song, panel chat with Johnny, second song
. . . instrumental number
TR . . . we'll pay transportation
L . . . we'll supply a limo
H . . . we'll pay hotel bill
4 off . . . there will be additional musicians off-stage
4 on . . . there will be backup musicians onstage
HM . . . we'll pay for special hair and makeup
ST . . . strings (violins) must be hired

On such days as sketches are scheduled, there will be pink cards reading:

MCAP . . . Mighty Carson Art Players
Blabby . . . Johnny as elderly woman
Carnac . . . Johnny as a Visitor from the East
Tea Time . . . the Art Fern character
Turbo . . . Johnny as the Bigot
Band # . . . Doc and the band will be featured

These cards and symbols tell me at a glance the exact status of tonight's show and the needs for the next thirty programs. Once I've assimilated the immediate and long-range situations, I'm ready for the phone call. It will come on my absolutely private line, it will arrive at exactly ten o'clock, and it will be from Johnny Carson. It is ten o'clock, my phone just rang, I'll have to get back to you folks shortly.

I'm considered a more than acceptable conversationalist, and you know that Johnny can inspire the dullest of guests to be fascinating, but you'd never know it from the ten o'clock phone communication. It rarely runs more than three minutes and will probably go something like this:

FRED: Will you identify yourself, please.

JOHN: Obviously I've dialed a disconnected number.

FRED: I thought you never made a mistake.

JOHN: Not since I hired you.

FRED: Now I recognize you! It's the Rajah of Rudeness.

JOHN: I don't have a hell of a lot of time for small talk. Who's on tonight?

FRED: You'll have a ball. The monologue, of course. I've read the sketch. You play Dr. Ruth Westheimer, and it's funny. Wardrobe and makeup are ready for you at one. Our first guest is a hundred-year-old woman who can touch the floor with the palms of her hands and wants to see if you can do it. Then it's David Letterman with a funny clip from his show, and we close with the world's greatest jazz guitarist, who will rehearse two numbers and will do one or two depending on how much time we have left.

JOHN: Is that enough show?

FRED: Unless someone helps us out by dropping dead, it's too much show.

JOHN: You always say that. Oh, did you read the new issue of *Modern Dentistry?*

FRED: No, mine must have been delayed in the mail.

JOHN: Get it. There's an article about a new technique where the patient doesn't even remember he's been to the office. It might make a funny sketch.

FRED: I'll read it right away, and maybe I'll go see that dentist and maybe I won't remember to be here for your call tomorrow.

JOHN: Make my day!

FRED: Anything else?

JOHN: I ask the questions! See you later.

I get copies of *Modern Dentistry,* give them to the writers, and three weeks later the suggestion turns into a funny sketch on the program.

But not all the phone calls are quite that lighthearted. One might sound like this:

FRED: Good morning, Johnny, how's everything?

JOHN: Did you read the article in —— this morning?

FRED: Yes, I did. It wasn't very flattering.

JOHN: Do you know the guy who wrote it?

FRED: No, but they tell me he's new and wants to make a name for himself by taking you on.

JOHN: Was he ever treated rudely by anyone on the staff?

FRED: Not that I know of.

JOHN: Make sure. Some of the stuff he wrote is true. We *do* use the same guests too often.

FRED: Come on, it's the nature of the beast.

There are actually only twenty really good guests in all the world.

JOHN: Bullshit. Tell the coordinators I want to meet with them today. We've got to dig deeper for new people.

FRED: I'll arrange it.

JOHN: If you run into that writer, tell him we read the article and didn't like it . . . but he made some good points.

FRED: About tonight's show—

JOHN: I'll be in early. We'll talk then.

FRED: There are a couple of things I'd like to discuss before then. . . .

Not much satisfaction in talking to a dead phone, is there?

It's 10:04—time flies when you're having fun. Reluctantly I view the cassettes. The chances are they will be a waste of time, but every once in a while . . . Most of them are music videos, overproduced and overorchestrated, so that there's no way to evaluate what the performer could do live on our show. Others are sent by agents and managers who represent such "undiscovered" talent as the eleven-year-old girl who "sings better than Garland ever did"; the country & western band who rope mechanical bulls while they sing; the eighty-year-old man who "does the best impersonation of Ed Sullivan you've ever seen"; or, much more sadly, the formerly rather important singing star who has straightened out his drinking problem and would love another shot on the program.

There's some ingenuity required in writing the letters that accompany the return of the cassettes—it's not nice to bruise the feelings of people who have enough problems as it is. It's even less nice to give too much encouragement when the eventual turndown is a foregone conclusion. Usually I thank the folks for their time and talent, explain that they shouldn't anticipate a booking, but we do send them our best wishes along with our regrets.

Of course, every once in a while there is the pleasant surprise—the never-before-heard-of comedian who is truly funny, the character who makes all sorts of jewelry out of quail droppings, and the winner of the turkey-calling contest, who sincerely believes in what he does. Every now and then even us blind hogs find us an acorn.

It's 10:40. Now it's time to open shop, to make some phone calls; time to find out if Sammy Davis, Jr., can fit us into his schedule before he opens in Las Vegas on the eighteenth. I call his confidante, Shirley Rhodes, firm up a date (song, panel chat with Johnny, second song), and send our best to Sammy's wife, Altovise. I get through to Bill Cosby, who's always pleasant and funny, hasn't a day open for a long time to come. What with his hit series, his nightclub appearances, and his commercials, it's "no" at this moment. He sends his best to Johnny. Beverly Sills has to cancel her trip West, so can't be with us, as planned, on the twenty-fifth. She's sorry and will let us know, well in advance, the next time she'll be out our way. She hopes we're not mad—no, but we are disappointed. Michael Caine will be available to us on the eighteenth, nineteenth, or twenty-fifth. He's sorry he couldn't confirm earlier, but he just received his new shooting schedule. We agree on the nineteenth and we're glad; he's always a welcome guest.

I really should look over the comedy spot the writers have left on my desk, but it's 11:00 and that's when the coordinators meet with me to share the victories and defeats of the day. I push a button, a bell rings throughout the complex, and it's time to put on a happy face.

Shirley, Bob, Jim, Debbie, and Darcy troop into my

office carrying their "booking books" and their notes about possibilities who have emerged since last we met. Peter will be in later; he's in his office on the phone, talking to the managers of Jay Leno, Garry Shandling, and Billy Crystal about the guests they think would be great when their "guys" host in three weeks. Each of the coords goes to the chair that has been established as his or hers. Each chair has a phone next to it so that calls can be transferred to my office. For a solid hour it's a no-holds-barred discussion of everything that can hurt or help our programming.

We start by going over the show for tonight: who will go on first (and has to be a "good-bye" because she's catching a plane for Reno, where she opens later tonight); who hasn't been available for a pre-interview (which means the topics of the interview with Johnny will have to be "spitballed"); how much time should be allotted to each guest for his area of conversation to "hold up"; what time the singer will arrive for rehearsal; the concern that the comedian's routine may be a little too raunchy; who has insisted there be no discussion about his romance with the leading lady of his most recent picture; and whose car was totaled last night and can't get here unless we send a limo.

Okay, we have analyzed our situation for tonight. Now we turn our attention to the never-ending future —or at least the next two weeks. Why has Bruce Willis turned us down? Is he really that busy? Or that sick? Or is he just plain ducking us? Isn't there anyone new and interesting anyone's been able to turn up? What plays and pictures are opening soon? Who is in them and who, in addition to being a splendid performer, can open his mouth? And why is Sally Field, who is up for an award and appearing all over the tube, unable to fit us into her busy schedule? And why can't we find more civilians like the lady who thought salted nuts were a major factor in sexual fulfillment?

It may help you to understand this meeting if I point out that each of the coords has been assigned to cover, or has insisted on handling, an exclusive area. Each has one or two movie studios; each has certain public relations firms, theaters, nightclubs, talent agencies, publishing houses, record companies. The whole pie has been divided equally. In addition, certain stars "belong" to certain coords who have learned, over the years, their needs, their eccentricities, and their closest contacts.

And the *Yellow Pages* won't help a lot when you want to get through to a star. But we have some channels that do help. Evelyn—Michael Landon's secretary—is the only one who can give you the actual availability of the man. She knows when he's due to finish his TV shows and if he's taking off on one of his "there's-no-way-to-reach-Mr.-Landon" vacations. No one will even know where he is—but Evelyn does.

It's okay to call Shelley Winters at home. Be prepared to put your life on hold while she tells you, in detail, about her most recent misadventures and triumphs. But, for us, it is worth it.

Tony will cut through the red tape and the battery of Julio's closest friends when you want to reach Julio Iglesias. Mr. Charm may not be due in our area for the next six months, but Tony says that we can count on him for October 25. Three songs and we'll need seven violins plus our band.

Charles Nelson Reilly can't be reached by phone. You have to leave a letter under his doormat; he'll call back as soon as he looks under the mat. He's often out of town for a month or so, which means that your messages may turn out to be a bit dated.

Alan King gives you his New York office and home phone numbers. If he's headed our way for "film confabs," he'll agree to arrive a day early or stay a day longer if it will help us. It often does and he always scores.

Rodney Dangerfield's secretary/manager keeps score for us. He won't do the show until he has twenty-five new jokes he thinks are especially good. We've pointed out that we'll take twenty new jokes and five old ones. But he has his standards.

Judy Tannen is in charge of Steve Lawrence and Eydie Gorme—and I mean *in charge*. "Her" singers are often on tour, but she can tell you their movements: where they are appearing, what they ate for breakfast, how their records are selling, and who is coming for dinner.

Irving Fein speaks for George Burns. George does exactly what Irving says—if George feels like it. Irving handled the show-business life of Jack Benny for years, he now is the confidant of George Burns, and rumor has it that he has his eye on Red Skelton. Not exactly a baby-boomer.

We know that it is a waste of our time and theirs to pursue a certain group of stars we'd love to have on the show. They've said "no, thanks" time and again:

Woody Allen	Jack Nicholson
Al Pacino	Meryl Streep
Dustin Hoffman	Paul Newman
Jessica Lange	Katharine Hepburn
Robert Redford	Anne Bancroft
Robert De Niro	John Gielgud

They all give us a polite "Not at this time" even if at dinner the night before they've said, "It might be fun; let me think about it and I'll get back to you." A large number of them may be making the right decision. After all, great stardom in itself doesn't guarantee an ability to provide amusing conversation if one has to create it without the assistance of an author or playwright. There are exceptions, of course. Or are there?

All of us are constantly aware of the problems we face in the overall scheme of guest-getting. The fact remains, however, that we have to fill a minimum of three spots every night. Accomplishing that task might go something like this:

FRED: Shirley, any chance of putting together an animal spot with either Jim Fowler or Joan Embery? It's been three months since the tarantula crawled up Johnny's sleeve.

SHIRLEY: Don't count on it. Fowler is out of the country and won't be back for a month. Joan says she's fresh out of animals who haven't starred on our show. She's got three chimps who are still too nervous, and there's a tiger who should be audience-ready soon. Give her a month and she'll have a good spot.

FRED: It's been almost a year since we've done the Singing Dog Follies. Audiences always love it.

SHIRLEY: I knew you'd think of that. Okay, ask Johnny to mention on the air that it's time for dog owners to write in or call me about their performing dogs and I'll start getting it together. Give me six weeks to organize it. This will be the twelfth time we've done it. I can handle the dogs—but oh, the owners!

FRED: Anything new on Aretha Franklin? She has a new album being released next month.

SHIRLEY: I'll call. But you know that she won't fly. Even if she's available, we'll have to bring her out by train and then put her up at a hotel for two days while she recovers from Amtrak lag.

FRED: Try to get her. What about Raquel Welch?

SHIRLEY: Will you take her daughter with her? I think she may insist.

FRED: Just check availability and find out if anyone can give you a line on the girl—she's pretty enough. Anyone else in mind?

SHIRLEY: What are your feelings about Drew Barrymore? She was cute and natural last time. Want to try her again?

FRED: Talk to her on the phone. You can tell if she's still cute or has turned into a smartass. If she's okay, I'll check with Johnny. Keep going.

SHIRLEY: Brooke Shields has just graduated from college. Her mother said they might be coming West.

FRED: Find out if she'd rather do the show with John or a guest host. It's okay either way. Anyone else?

SHIRLEY: Not too much. Peter Falk is shooting a picture in Florida and he's got marriage problems. His wife might be a better guest. John Houseman is rehearsing a play in New York and thinks Johnny is zinging him too much in the monologue.

FRED: Carl Reiner? Rob Reiner?

SHIRLEY: One's directing a picture in Europe; the other's directing a picture in Alaska. I guess it runs in the family.

FRED: Pictures eventually finish. Get dates. Dudley Moore?

SHIRLEY: I snared him at Spago. He'll do us on the twenty-first and will play the piano.

FRED: Good work. I'll pick up your tab at Spago.

SHIRLEY: I know. I signed your name.

FRED: Okay, Bobby [that's Dolce], you're in the barrel.

DOLCE: Here's the rundown. If I make one more phone call to Susan Sarandon, she'll kill me.

She won't come West just to do the show. If she gets a picture out here, she'll do us. Ann-Margret ran into Johnny at La Scala and will come aboard if she can think of anything to say. I told her I'd make up something. She wasn't impressed.

FRED: Jane Fonda? Dyan Cannon?

DOLCE: Jane will be in Europe for another month, but she's got a new exercise cassette coming out soon. Dyan is on her honeymoon. When she returns, if the marriage is intact, we'll get her. In the meantime, she wants to thank Johnny for the lavish wedding gift. Diana Ross is set for the fifteenth. I agreed to airfare, limo, hairdresser, makeup, and first-guest position. She'll do a medley and panel.

FRED: Robert Klein?

DOLCE: I'll call, but I think he's doing the college circuit.

FRED: There are colleges out here, too.

DOLCE: He'll be delighted to learn that.

FRED: Anything else?

DOLCE: Lots. There is a lady who owns a trained pig. She says it can do anything a dog can do. It lives in her house; it's potty-trained; and she loves it.

FRED: So it's a first-class pig. Is the lady liable to be an interesting guest?

DOLCE: She owns a trained pig, she says it can do anything a dog can do, she potty-trained it, the pig lives in her house . . . and you ask me if she'll be an interesting guest!

FRED: Okay, I'm sold.

DOLCE: It's not that simple—the pig won't fly.

FRED: Pigs aren't supposed to fly.

DOLCE: No wonder you get the big money! I'll see how it feels about automobiles.

FRED (TO MCCAWLEY): Jimbo, it's been a year since Robin Williams has been on. What's the problem?

JIM: He's living on some goddamn farm up north, he has a new baby, and he says he'll do our show if he does *any* show but we shouldn't hold our breath. On the other hand, George Carlin is ready to—

At this point Peter Lassally walks into the office with a batch of notes in his hand. I should point out that he's the show's main man on guest-host bookings.

Peter stays close to the camps of all the folks who sit in for Johnny. It isn't that these folks dislike me; it's simply that they appreciate the amount of time and interest Peter devotes to their concerns and their suggestions. In the meantime, I have Johnny's high regard to keep me warm.

Most of our replacement hosts in '87—Bill Cosby, Kenny Rogers, Betty White, Billy Crystal, Garry Shandling, Jay Leno, Patrick Duffy, and Chevy Chase so far this year—work and think differently from Carson. J.C. uses three guests; they feel safer with four. Some do opening monologues; others do not. Johnny doesn't sing, and some of them do. In short, it's a whole new ball game when Carson's on vacation. And on the weeks when we use different guest hosts every night, it's five new ball games. That can sometimes feel like a complete season.

As their fateful appearance day approaches, I move in and explain the details of the job and try to ease the last-minute jitters. Until then we, through Peter, evaluate their guest suggestions in the light of our lengthy *Tonight Show* background. Happily they realize how important that input is. Just remember the last time your wife made all the dinner invitations without discussing the cast of characters with you!

FRED: Okay, Pete, what's on their minds?

PETER: Here's a list of people they'd like: New York City's Mayor Ed Koch.

SHIRLEY: He's very witty and prepared. And he has a book to plug. I'll check his availability.

PETER: Gloria Vanderbilt?

FRED: I had dinner with her last week and I doubt that she'll do it with anyone but Johnny, but Lazar says she can handle herself with anyone, so let's give it a try. After all, it's important to her to keep the book on the *Times*'s Top Ten list.

PETER: Linda Evans?

JIM: I'll make her the offer for one of the guest hosts. She just was on with Johnny.

FRED: Please tell her that I think she's lovely.

PETER: I'm sure that will make her day. Joan Collins?

SHIRLEY: She's been on everything and never fails to make it work. It might be fun if she and Linda were on together.

PETER: Rich Little?

FRED: You know how I feel about impressionists in general. Rich, Gorshin, Travalena, Anderson —they're all talented, but how long can they go on doing Cagney, Stewart, Lancaster, Reagan, Nixon, Carter, and Kirk Douglas? Let's hold off on that area.

PETER: George Segal?

SHIRLEY: I'll check on him. Okay if he wants to play a banjo number with his group?

PETER: Sure.

FRED: I think people forget what a good actor he is.

PETER: Barbara Walters?

FRED: It's sure to work—she can handle anyone, including Godzilla, and be attractive at the same time.

PETER: What's the story on Dom DeLuise?

DEBBIE: He's making another picture with Burt Reynolds—*Cannonball Twenty-six*. When it's finished, we'll get him and Burt . . . or Burt and him.

PETER: How about Liza Minnelli?

FRED: Get her—if she'll sing. Otherwise the audience feels cheated. You present a singer, you expect a song.

PETER: Lionel Richie?

JIM: He's talented, likes to do our show, sends his regards to Johnny, and will be available in 1989 . . . possibly.

FRED: Peter, use your judgment. If any of those folks are available, go with them. And check on the Young Turks—Tom Cruise, Michael J. Fox, Tom Hanks, Rob Lowe. And the Female Turks—Justine Bateman, Demi Moore, Molly Ringwald; they might feel more at ease with a guest host than with Johnny. And let's waste one more phone call on Clint Eastwood.

PETER: Will do. How are you folks doing for Johnny?

FRED: Just fair. Will you take over? I want to check Johnny's comedy-material spot for tonight's show. I'll be in your office if you want me. (I leave, but the meeting goes on. Later Peter gives me an update.)

PETER: Jim, I know you're staying on top of Eddie Murphy. Anything new?

JIM: Not really. He's breaking records on tour. His people say he'll do the show when his new picture comes out, and he'll do us first. He likes Johnny . . . and he doesn't like everyone in the world.

PETER: When does the new picture go into release?

JIM: As soon as he finishes counting his take from his last picture—a dollar at a time. That could take a little while.

PETER: What about Richard Pryor?

JIM: I talk to his folks about once a week. He's deep into his new picture and is a little nervous about it. The movie company thinks it's a big one and is anxious to have him appear. You know how shy he is, but I'd say he'll be with us before long.

PETER: What about the new comics?

JIM: I've got three who are just about ready. Jerry Seinfeld has a new seven minutes that will really work, Kevin Nealon is my first choice, and Fat Louie Anderson needs one more night at the Improv and he'll be great.

PETER: Steven Wright did the Share Benefit Show Saturday night and they say he was the hit of the show. We could use him between Charles Grodin and that pretty Courteney Cox on the fifteenth.

JIM: I don't think so. His routine was pretty much what he did on our show two weeks ago. Let's hold off for a few weeks until he develops some new stuff.

PETER: We'll get to you in a minute, Deb, but I want to check something with you, Shirl. You and Fred saw a videotape of the pianist Horacio Gutierrez and agreed he should be booked. The "board" says he'll be in town next week.

SHIRLEY: The audience will love him. He can do six to ten minutes and he can talk. He'll be a smash—I guarantee it.

PETER: See what's the best night for him and lock him in. He speaks English, doesn't he?

SHIRLEY: He did when I talked to him last Tuesday.

PETER: Okay, Deb, you're on.

DEBBIE: Vanity. She won't have her group with her, but I think she'll turn Johnny on. He wants new faces and she's got one, plus a new body. She's a bit bizarre, but I think it's worth a shot.

PETER: You're sure she's not just a bimbo?

DEBBIE: She's young, she's hot, and she's attractive. I didn't say she's Mother Teresa.

PETER: If she dies, she dies. Book her.

I return about now, not very happy at the spot the writers have come up with for tonight. It's funny enough, but it's a lot like something we did a few nights ago. I'll go into that later. Back to the booking problems.

FRED: Have you discussed the usuals—Melissa Manchester, Linda Ronstadt, Barry Manilow, Rod Stewart, Cyndi Lauper, Tina Turner?

DEBBIE: I've got a date on Cyndi, and Manilow says okay the night before he opens at the amphitheater, Tina Turner may do it on New Year's Eve, Rod is a flat no, and I just can't get anything from Linda. But I saw a new girl last night. She's got two numbers in the Top Twenty. She's gospel-oriented and she's nervous about doing us because we're not. Her name is Amy Grant, and I told her I've just been born again.

FRED: Can I see a video of her in action?

DEBBIE: In my office after the meeting?

FRED: Right. Pete, how do you think Johnny will react to the Oak Ridge Boys? They scored last time.

PETER: Performance only, sure, but not if they want to panel with John.

FRED: Okay, Jim, call Halsey and book them.

JIM: What if they insist on "sitting down"?
FRED: Tell them all the seats are taken. Okay,
let's break this meeting up. I'm worried about
the comedy spot for tonight. I think we may
have to go to "Stumpies" or "Blue Cards."

"Stump the Band" is our backup, and always reliable, follow-the-monologue segment when Johnny decides that what the writers have come up with isn't strong enough. He's been doing it for years and enjoys it. Our in-studio audience gets a chance to be involved in the show, and our at-home audiences get a chance to see Johnny at his unrehearsed best. He goes into the audience, asks three or four people at random if they know, and can sing, a song the band won't know. They "name that tune"; the band (fronted by Ed and Doc) does or doesn't know it. If not, the guest sings a portion of the song, is given chits for a dinner for four or six at a fashionable restaurant, and everyone is delighted. The byplay between Johnny and the participant is invariably entertaining, and the writers realize they'll have to work a little harder the next day.

"Blue Cards" is another substitute for a written spot that we feel may not be worth the effort. Blue $3'' \times 5''$ cards are distributed to the folks standing in line waiting to get into the studio for the show. They are asked to write their names, where they come from, and a question they would like to ask Johnny Carson. Right after the monologue, I give these cards to Johnny and he reads the question, identifies the writer, and answers the query. His ability to amuse, off the cuff, never ceases to fascinate me.

I'm sure it will be "Blue Cards" or "Stumpies" tonight unless Johnny decides the written material will work, and I'll argue against it. It's now noon and time for the production meeting. I push the button again, the coords remain, and a new group joins us.

This gathering of eagles comprises the most efficient and disrespectful group of technicians in the television business. They were not selected, as was the Dirty Dozen, to accomplish a hazardous mission; nor did they band together by accident. They are delighted to be on our program. I should explain: *The Tonight Show* has no season; we operate fifty-two weeks a year, as opposed to even the most successful prime-time programs. Those shows tape, at the most, thirty episodes a year. There is, therefore, a twenty-two-week salary differential. Also, we do not go on location to the frozen North or the blazing Sahara. We have, I admit, crossed Catalina Avenue to Buena Vista Park (fifty yards from the NBC parking lot) on two or three occasions, but that's our most distant location. The continuity of salary and the comforts of home have gathered to us a contented and most efficient group of workers. We, and they, are pleased.

The group at the noon meeting is made up of the heads of all the departments responsible for the actual taping of the program. Bobby Quinn is their leader and he is responsible for their efforts. Included are the scenic designer, the wardrobe mistress, the sound technicians, the property master, the musical coordinator, makeup and hairdressing bosses, the NBC liaison, the assistant director, the technical director, the stage managers, the cost evaluator, the commercial producer, and Johnny's very attractive secretary, Drue Ann Wilson. The meeting is called to make sure that all eventualities for the night's performance are understood. Everyone is expected to listen carefully to all the elements of the show, not just their own, so that a complete picture of the evening's activities will be clear. The meeting is over in twenty minutes, and the morning's work is done. It's lunchtime.

Lunch break for the staff, when you're running a big-time operation like *The Tonight Show,* must be a gay (in the old sense of the word), fascinating two-hour three-martini interlude spent in some fascinating bistro among the elite. Well, let me tell you the pure, unvarnished truth—no way!

Everyone is completely free from parental supervision for exactly one hour. Carson, who believes that the lunch break is an unwarranted intrusion on the decent activities of the day, feels that one hour is more than enough of a midday wastage. After all, how long can it take even the most inept person to eat a ham-and-cheese sandwich, no matter how heavy it may be on the mayo?

So the technicians disappear as per union rules and quickly reappear on the stage of Studio One to prepare for tonight's eventualities. That means that they must check every light, every mike, every prop, every piece of wardrobe, every clock, every set, every dressing room, every headset.

The coords mostly brown-bag-it in their offices and "waste" the rest of their lunchtime

(a) reading and answering their mail;

(b) investigating the values, and lack thereof, of possible future bookings;

(c) viewing cassettes;

(d) returning phone calls;

(e) preparing their notes for tonight's guests;

(f) gathering in a sullen communal group to discuss and complain about their treatment by Fred and Peter.

Fred and Peter, however, secure in the knowledge that all is in capable hands, lunch together as they have *every day* since they started working together seventeen years ago. In New York and out here in California we have arranged our private lives and our business schedules so that from 12:30 to 1:30 we can be alone for evaluation. Distanced from the blandishments and the pressures of the outside world, for one brief, shining hour we can try to put it all into perspective. On rare occasions when illness crops up or vacations interfere, one of us may not be available to the other. But otherwise we show up at our corner table in the Hungry Peacock (the fabled NBC commissary), which isn't exactly the West Coast version of "21" but is considerably better than the Carson monologues might lead you to believe.

Our constant luncheon relationship has, I'm told, given rise to base rumors about our personal relationship. I can only state, in rebuttal, that Peter supports a loving wife and two charming adult children, and I support a loving wife and a coterie of the nation's most respected clothing creators and the number one hairdresser and very dear friend, Yuki.

If, then, we are "in the clear," what can we possibly have to talk about day after day? Primarily the show. There is some discussion about our respective lives—our families, whom we went out with last night and where, Peter's children and houseguests, my golf game—all of which takes about ten minutes. For the rest of the hour we brief each other about what we've heard or read or seen that might have some impact on our show. We evaluate Johnny's current mood, people we've watched on competing programs, the newest crop of "instant stars" who will be appearing on the upcoming premiere episodes of the season's new and improved programs, and the folks we saw last night at Spago or Morton's or the Bistro Garden. We don't have to discuss Chasen's—the same stalwarts, led by Jimmy Stewart, will always be there. Obviously, it all relates to *The Tonight Show*. And strangely enough, it is never boring—because the program is the mirror image of all our lives.

There's another plus: we regularly bump into various stars who are taping their shows in nearby studios at NBC—Bob Hope, George Burns, Jack Lemmon, Dean Martin, Johnny Mathis, Jim Garner, Loni Anderson, Ann Jillian, Pat Sajak, Victoria Principal, and the ever-popular and ever-changing soap-opera stars. And in spite of all the years we've been in the business, we feel pleased to be part of this exciting world.

It's 1:30. We tape the show at 5:30. Four hours till show time and the real work is still to be done. We see that Carson's Corvette is in his assigned parking place —number one, the nearest to the artists' entrance. He's on time, of course. But we don't go to see him. We wait for the telephoned message that ''Johnny is ready for you.'' We know that until that summons is received, he is editing and revising his gospel—The Monologue according to Saint John.

And the Beat
Goes On

Back in the office, I find that another mail delivery has resulted in a new batch of video cassettes, press-agent "pushes," the happy news that two firmly booked guests for next week have schedule problems and must cancel, and that we have an air-conditioning problem at home. All but the last I can handle. And I know for sure that the warranty on our cooling system will have expired yesterday and a heat wave is on the way.

Pressing on, I visit each coordinator and gather the notes they have prepared for Carson on tonight's guests. Although ours is a totally ad-lib program, it could, without an agenda, become a staring contest. To make sure that doesn't happen, the coord chats with his or her assigned guest and comes up with a list of areas that, hopefully, will lead to interesting and provocative conversation. The guests thereby know what subjects Johnny is liable to discuss and he, in turn, knows that the guest will be prepared with answers to his questions. At least that's the theory.

Actually, the notes act as a security blanket for both guest and host. Both know they are available if needed, but many of our most fascinating segments have resulted from a question or an answer out of the blue.

But the notes and the rundown are delivered to Johnny for each show to insure that he is completely familiar with our plans for the Bewitching Hour.

I now present you the rundowns of two of our shows so that you, in the safety of your home, can see what Johnny has in front of him when he finishes his monologue and sits down at the desk.

He'll find before him: three pencils with erasers at both ends, a cup containing apple juice, a cigarette box, a lighter, and a legal size manila folder.

Inside the folder will be: the order in which the guests will appear: 5 × 7 introduction cards indicating their upcoming concert appearances or the date their books will be published or their albums released or their most recent movie will appear in "theaters throughout the country." The cards will also contain such pertinent information as will make the audience more familiar with the history and triumphs of the guests' past. Also, for everyone appearing on the show (unless the booking is "performance only") there will be a series of questions and, in some instances, some of the answers that can be expected.

You now have Johnny's tools and it's time to make your choice—you can pretend you are about to host *The Tonight Show* or just sit back and enjoy it.

THE TONIGHT SHOW   5/21/85

GUESTS:	Sylvester Stallone
	A. Whitney Brown
	Horacio Gutierrez
HOST:	Johnny Carson
ANNCR:	Ed McMahon
COND:	Doc Severinsen

5:30 for 11:30 airing	6:00 for 12:00 airing

1. Theme and opening music
2. Johnny: Monologue
3. Comml: (two at $45,000 per ½ minute)
4. Comedy Material: Public Service Announcements
5. Comml: (2 more)
6. Sylvester Stallone
7. Comml: (2 more)
8. (Station Identification)

9. Theme Music #2
10. Sylvester Stallone with clip from *Rambo*
11. Comml: (2 more)
12. A. Whitney Brown (monologue only)
13. Comml: (2 more)
14. Horacio Gutierrez (piano number, panel, 2nd number if desired)
15. Comml: (2 more)
16. Goodnights (to audience and guests)
17. Promo: Tomorrow's Guests

SCRIPT (5/21/85)

Public Service Announcement

JOHNNY (SETUP)

When you're a celebrity, a lot of charitable groups, civic organizations, government agencies, and groups like that ask you to donate your time to tape public service announcements for them. Well, I agreed to tape a few public service announcements today. Now, I usually come in early before the show to do these spots. I didn't have time today because I was running late. So I'm gonna ask your indulgence while I run through these public service announcements right now, and then we'll go on with the rest of the show.

Here's how it works. The various agencies send

over copy, which is put on cue cards. Please bear with me, because I haven't even had the chance to read the copy, so I'll be doing these spots . . . what they say in show business "cold."

I'm sorry I have to do this now, but at least you'll have a chance to see how all these public service announcements that you see on television are done.

The United States Naval Academy

You know, here in America we've drilled our oil, mined our coal, and even harnessed the energy from the sun. But there's one vast natural resource we've completely overlooked. Belly-button lint. As a fuel, it's very efficient. Did you know that the button residue from one fat man can keep a family of four warm all winter? And as a fabric, it's fantastic. This stylish dress shirt I'm wearing is woven from one hundred percent natural tummy textiles. For ideas on how you too can help our country eliminate our reliance on foreign sheep, call . . .

. . . The United States Naval Academy, 1-800-555-LINT.

Kilt Without Guilt

Hi, this is Johnny Carson with a word about a forgotten minority out there. Shy Scotsmen. As you know, when men from Scotland wear their distinctive national garment, they have nothing on underneath. Now, this doesn't bother most of them at all, but for a timid few, it's a living hell. Especially if they make their living as tightrope walkers or skylight installers. These men need psychological counseling. Send your contribution today to . . .

. . . Kilt Without Guilt, Glasgow, Scotland. Let them know that there's nothing bad under the plaid.

Parrots Without Partners

You know, if there's one thing I've learned in my lifetime it's this. You're not likely to get lucky if one of your legs is chained to a perch and there's a sick St. Bernard puppy throwing up in the cage next to you. That's the dilemma faced each and every day by the talking birds in America's pet stores. But if you've got a feathered friend, you can help. Stuff your bird in an envelope and mail it to . . .

. . . Parrots Without Partners, Squawk, Wisconsin. Do it today, because Polly wants more than a cracker.

Fly the Scary Skies

Johnny Carson asking all you high school kids out there: Do you have a summer job lined up? Well, instead of mowing lawns and busing dishes for peanuts, how'd you like to pocket a fast seventy-five grand? How? It's easy. Just dye your sideburns gray and go to the United Airlines gate at your local airport. As long as you have a driver's license, or even a learner's permit, they'll put you to work immediately as a pilot. Why spend your summer cruising Main Street when you could be cruising at thirty-five thousand feet and terrifying three hundred passengers to boot? Come on, kids. Help United . . .

. . . fly the scary skies.

I Like Ike and Sonny

Hi, this is Johnny Carson. You know, I guess the two hottest ladies in show business today are Tina Turner and Cher. But we haven't heard much lately from their ex-husbands. These two guys have a whole lot of entertaining left in them. So why not team 'em up for an album of their own? If you agree with me, send your letter of support to . . .

. . . I Like Ike and Sonny, Capitol Records Building, Hollywood, California.

Stamp Out DMV-D

Hi, I'm Johnny Carson asking if you're aware of the number-one method of transmitting social disease in this country. The number-one method of transmitting social disease is that little pencil attached to the string on the counter of the Department of Motor Vehicles. This pencil should be regularly replaced or at least sprayed occasionally with disinfectant. Write to the director of your state's Department of Motor Vehicles and urge him to . . .

. . . stamp out DMV-D.

Guest Interview # 1
Intro for SYLVESTER STALLONE

My first guest is that rare breed—an accomplished actor, writer and director. He's currently starring in *Rambo: First Blood, Part Two,* which opens tomorrow. Would you please welcome . . . SYLVESTER STALLONE!

As a youth you were expelled from three schools as a troublemaker. What kind of trouble would you get yourself into?

I heard that in grade school you believed you were Superboy, that you wore his shirt under your school clothes.

You said that when you were in New York you'd lost out on what seemed like five thousand auditions. It was only when you thought you weren't going to make it as an actor that you started learning about writing.

You were broke then, and I heard you hung out in the library because it was warm.

You also slept on a bench in the Port Authority.

Your break came [in 1974] when you were cast in *The Lords of Flatbush*. Henry Winkler, Susan Blakely, and Perry King were in that movie, too. What did you talk to each other about?

Once again, you had to go through grueling physical training for *Rambo*. How many hours a week do you invest in keeping in shape?

You get rid of your fantasies on the screen. One of them was singing, which took five months of coaching.

In *Rambo* you get rid of another [that of the archer who used to shoot a golden arrow].

What are some of your other unfulfilled fantasies?

You've said you want to do a western, that you ride better than you do anything. Don't you think horses are dumb?

I hear you'll be doing *Rocky Four* with a Soviet giant.

People like to invent stories about you. What's your favorite?

Let's take a look at your film clip . . . It's a segment titled "Over the Cliff."

Intro to:
A. WHITNEY BROWN
(Guest #2 - no panel planned)

My next guest is a most talented young comedian. He will be appearing at Cobb's Pub in San Francisco May twenty-ninth to June first and at the San Diego Improvisation June fourth to June ninth.

Please welcome . . . A. WHITNEY BROWN.
STAND UP—6 minutes.
OUTCUE: "Thank you very much."

Intro to:
Horacio Gutierrez (Guest #3)

My next guest is very prominent in the world of classical music. He will be performing at Royce Hall, UCLA, on May twenty-third and at the Ambassador Auditorium on May twenty-sixth. He is featured in the "Mostly Mozart Festival, Live from Lincoln Center," which will be on public television on July tenth.

Please welcome . . . HORACIO GUTIERREZ!

FYI: (He'll perform piano solo, center stage, then join you at panel for interview)

GUTIERREZ QUESTIONS
  (Answers are indicated)

You had a piano delivered to the studio that you selected personally. Besides its sound, what else must be considered?

The sound, the tone, is most important, but so is the action of the keys when played. He always finds out who played the piano last, as there are players who tinker with them. To him, it's abusing a piano.

What can be done to a piano to change it?

Pianos have their own sound, which can't be changed, but certain pianists tinker with the mechanism so it plays easier. One person sprays hair spray on the keys so they aren't slippery. The keys have even been sand-papered by a person who has sweaty fingers. If he knows someone has done something to his piano, he gets very depressed if there's not an alternate instrument, or he works on the piano to suit himself. The next pianist will blame him for the mess.

Do you always know ahead of time if there's an acceptable instrument to play?

No, that's his biggest worry. When he arrives in town, he checks the piano before he checks into his room.

You are an American citizen, born in Cuba. When did you come to the States?

In 1962, two years after the Castro revolution. His family arranged to go to South America. When they left they could not take any money.

How did you manage to survive without any money?

His aunt hid twenty dollars in a jar of cream. In South America they had relatives with money. Finally got to Miami. There Cuban refugees were given food plus one hundred dollars a month.

Where did you go to school—in Miami?

No, the family came to L.A. He went to Hollywood High, and the class president was John Ritter. His parents live in Burbank.

You play only classical music. It is possible, isn't it, for a concert to get boring?

Yes, the audience coughs a lot, ladies go through their purses, and it's generally restless. So far he's been lucky: there haven't been too many coughs—unless he's not been hearing them.

Do you ever play popular music for your own enjoyment?

Loves popular tunes from Broadway musicals but would never play them in his concerts; it would be like serving an elegant French dinner and throwing in chop suey.

(Reminder: he has rehearsed a second number, if we need it.)

Dear Reader—perhaps you'd rather host this show!

THE TONIGHT SHOW

GUESTS:	Luciano Pavarotti
	Bobby Kelton
	Vanna White
HOST:	Johnny Carson
ANNCR:	Ed McMahon
COND:	Doc Severinsen

5:30 for 11:30 airing   *6:00 for 12:00 airing*

1. Theme and opening music
2. Johnny: Monologue
3. Comml: 1 and 2
4. Comedy Material: Jokes Between the States
5. Comml: 3 and 4
6. Luciano Pavarotti (song to panel)
7. Comml: 5 and 6
8. (Station Identification)

9. Theme music #2
10. Pavarotti (cont.) (more panel to second song)
11. Comml: 7 and 8
12. Bobby Kelton (monologue only)
13. Comml: 9 and 10
14. Vanna White
15. Comml: 11 and 12 (still at $45,000 per ½ minute)
16. Goodnights (to guests and audience)
17. Promo: Tomorrow's Guests

SCRIPT (9/4/86)

Joke Rivalry Between the States

JOHNNY (SETUP)

Some time ago there was an article in the *Los Angeles Times* about the Great Midwestern Joke War that's now raging between Iowa and Minnesota. Apparently there's an intense rivalry between the two states, and the residents are doing put-down jokes about one another.

For example, they like to ask in Minnesota why all football fields in Iowa have artificial turf. It's so the cheerleaders won't graze after the game.

And in Iowa they're asking why Minnesotans don't drink more Kool-Aid. That's because they can't figure out how to get two quarts of water into one of those little paper envelopes.

The Iowa–Minnesota rivalry is only one rivalry. There are other rivalries between neighboring states that have been percolating for many years. We have some letters sent in to us by people from all over the country who apparently really feel hostility toward their neighboring states.

Oregon and Washington

In Oregon they say:

"What do you call a Washington State man wearing a suit?"

"The deceased."

In Washington they say:

"How can you tell who's the widow at an Oregon funeral?"

"She's the one hitting on the pallbearers."

Tennessee and Alabama

In Tennessee they say:

> *"What's the similarity between Alabama cars and Alabama formal dinners?"*

"Neither has plates."

In Alabama they say:

> *"Describe foreplay in Tennessee."*

"Honey, tell your brother to turn his back."

Ohio and Pennsylvania

In Ohio they say:

> *"In Pennsylvania on Halloween, what do women put on to scare kids at the door?"*

"The porch light."

In Pennsylvania they say:

> *"What are prostitutes officially charged with by Ohio police?"*

"Visa, MasterCard, American Express . . ."

Indiana and Michigan

In Indiana they say:

> *"Why have so many men in Michigan quit smoking?"*

"Their inflatable women kept exploding."

In Michigan they say:

> *"What do the women in Indiana call the local house of ill repute?"*

"Finishing school."

Florida and Georgia

In Florida they say:

> "What do most drivers in Georgia forget to buckle?"

"Their pants."

In Georgia they say:

> "Why don't women in Florida have to wear seat belts?"

"The damage has already been done."

North Dakota and South Dakota

In North Dakota they say:

> "In South Dakota, what do family members toss when they see the bride and groom coming out of a church?"

"Their cookies."

In South Dakota they say:

> "How does a North Dakota husband know when his wife's in the mood to make love?"

"He spots her car parked outside a motel."

Wisconsin and Illinois

In Wisconsin they say:

> "Why does an Illinois man occasionally need time to himself?"

"So he can make love."

In Illinois they say:

"In Wisconsin, what has six legs, moves very fast, and is usually found crawling out of bedroom windows?"

"The milkman, the mailman, and the paper boy."

Guest Interview #1
Intro for LUCIANO PAVAROTTI

My first guest is one of the finest tenors in the world today. He will be performing in Salt Lake City on September ninth, at the Rosemont Horizon in Chicago September twelfth, and at Madison Square Garden on September sixteenth. He will be singing here at the Hollywood Bowl September sixth with Dame Joan Sutherland. His latest album is called *Pavarotti Anniversary*.

Please welcome . . . LUCIANO PAVAROTTI.

JC: (FYI) Luciano has lots of stories. These questions should lead to amusing answers.

This year was the twenty-fifth anniversary of your opera debut. Does it seem that long?

We have a photo [Johnny holds up] taken some years ago showing you without a beard. When and why did you grow a beard?

There's a new book out this month about you that says you are an avid poker player. Are you any good?

It's difficult to imagine you with a poker face.

Another interest of yours is tennis. How's your game? [Johnny holds up a second photo, this time of Luciano playing tennis using his racquet in a weird fashion.]

When you travel, do you always take a tennis racquet and clothes, hoping for a game?

You had the big birthday last year in October. Do

you believe your sign, Libra, describes you accurately?

Your colleague, Placido Domingo, was on the show last month. How would you describe his voice?

Would you say there was a dramatic absence of tourists in Europe this summer?

FYI (Another song has been rehearsed.)

Intro to:
BOBBY KELTON (Guest #2)
(no panel planned)

My next guest is a funny young comedian who will be appearing next week at the Punchline in San Francisco and in mid-October at Gallagher's in Winnipeg, Canada.

Please welcome . . . BOBBY KELTON.

Intro to:
VANNA WHITE (Guest # 3)

My next guest is the resident letter turner on TV's highest rated game show, *Wheel of Fortune*. It's a pleasure to welcome . . . VANNA WHITE.

FYI: The producers of *Wheel* wouldn't let go of the contestant quiz questions, which she'd hoped to test you on. But she has plenty to talk about. Here are some areas she's prepared for.

Is it true that you once clapped so hard for a contestant that you fell on your face coming down the stairs of the puzzle platform?

She'll tell you what the contestant said after she made a slow and embarrassing recovery.

You were selected over two hundred applicants as the hostess of *Wheel*. What do you suppose you have that the others didn't?

They liked the way she turned the letters.

Did you have to learn those poses or did you make them up?

She'll elaborate.

When you were barely out of your teens, you just packed yourself up in a U-Haul and headed for California.

She didn't know "anything or anybody" and soon found out that "becoming a star" wasn't like it was supposed to be. She'll tell you about the day she became five foot seven.

In high school you were in just about everything.

She says: "All those years of cheerleading practice paid off."

You were a contestant in a lot of beauty pageants, including Miss Fire Prevention.

She always "placed" and never won and admits that she was "definitely disappointed at the time."

When you were asked which was your favorite vowel, did you really tell a reporter, "It's between the A and the E"?

She did, but she thought he knew she was joking.

You also said you have the ugliest toes in the world.

They're long and skinny.

Is fishing still one of your favorite activities?

She likes fresh-water fishing in Lake Michigan and says, "For some reason I get seasick on the ocean."

I heard that the only music you don't like is opera.

FYI: Pavarotti will be seated next to her and will probably react in mock dismay.

You're always immaculately groomed. I'm told that you took offense when a magazine said, "At home she's a slob."

She says: "Imagine them calling me a slob just 'cause I wear jeans."

Step by Step
(Continued)

When Billie notifies me that Johnny is "ready for us," I take the notes, the rundown, and such letters, ratings, clippings, and viewers' suggestions and criticisms as have merit—and we're off to see the Wizard. Peter and I hop aboard my golf cart for the quarter-mile drive from the bungalow to Studio One (the permanent home of *The Tonight Show* and the Bob Hope Specials), where we descend the sixteen steps that lead to Johnny's compact, tasteful, functional, and rather luxurious headquarters, get a facial expression from Carson's office chief, Drue, indicating that all is serene and calm—or not so s. and c.—knock on the door, and enter the Hub.

This two o'clock meeting is ordinarily a relaxed and informal one. We waste as much as two or three minutes on small talk and drift, quickly, into twenty minutes on the details of the upcoming program. If there's a first-time guest scheduled, I explain who it is and why we thought he or she was a good choice. If music is involved and it's MOR (middle of the road), I'm ordinarily the spokesman: "This singer is young and

Johnny and I with a pair of acceptable "hoofers" (Gene Kelly and Fred Astaire) during a commercial break on *The Tonight Show*.

David Wolper listens as I thank the Academy and Johnny for my sixth Emmy.

attractive, she's opening at the amphitheater tomorrow night, but don't expect her to sparkle when you talk to her. She's not a nuclear physicist.'' If the music is classical or far out, Peter will take over and explain the merits of the booking. I'll then background the last guest: "He writes for *The New Yorker,* he has interesting restaurant misadventures, and he has humorous comments about the Washington scene.'' When we finish, we find out, too often, that Johnny knows as much about the guests as we do. His evaluations may differ.

Next, we go over the names of the people who are available in the near future, and here we run into the strongest resistance. So many talented and effective performers have been with us so often during the long history of the show. They have names—they are immediately recognized by our audiences—and they are qualified, but, by the law of diminishing returns, Johnny is less than enthusiastic about bringing them back. He feels that by booking them again, the show presents a "we've-done-this-before" image, and he might be right. However, I continue to point out that he should consider that none of us meets too many new friends who are more interesting than those we've known for years. And he continues to point out that I'm paid a large weekly stipend to solve that problem. The following list of names, and my evaluations, may interest you—Johnny's heard it often enough. These staples of *The Tonight Show* are regularly first-rate guests and ordinarily are available to us two or three times a year:

SUZANNE PLESHETTE

She's amusing, very outspoken, irreverent, gently bawdy, and she and her husband, Tommy Gallagher, are Carson friends.

MICHAEL LANDON

He's a star, a writer, a director, and a producer of one major television success after another. Some people think he's smug and arrogant. I don't think so. Neither does he.

JIMMY STEWART

Just about the last of the "real" movie stars still in action. In spite of all his years at the top he is never pretentious, always gracious to the staff, and a standing ovation is guaranteed—and deserved.

CLORIS LEACHMAN

A certified "daffodil." There's no way to know what she'll say or do. An Oscar and Emmy winner and one of the risks and joys of doing a live television show.

GORE VIDAL

Bright, bitter, perceptive, and articulate. When he's with us, TV isn't quite so much of a wasteland.

CARL SAGAN

Johnny's knowledge of astronomy and Carl's recognition of that knowledge combine to make textbook talk both interesting and informative. He's made "billions and billions" more popular than did the Rockefellers.

ERMA BOMBECK

One of the few writers who can talk as funny as they write. She has a rare talent for translating everyone's frustrations into comedic form.

TERI GARR

An attractive actress who doesn't think she is. She's a critic's favorite but always insecure—never feels she's been a good guest, though she always is. She projects the same qualities as Diane Keaton—whom we don't see much anymore.

BUDDY HACKETT

Possibly the funniest man of all. Very risqué in all other venues but very circumspect with us (except during commercials when we're off the air). He always has stories, not just jokes, and is a first-class dialectician. J.C. enjoys him as much as the audience does.

DAVID LETTERMAN

Clearly the most inventive of the new stars. *The Tonight Show* didn't discover him, but he quickly became one of the family. In spite of his sizable success, he remains totally in awe of Johnny.

ANGIE DICKINSON

The ultimate talk-show flirt—and possibly every man's secret desire. One of a small group equally popular with men and women, on screen and off.

STEVE LAWRENCE AND EYDIE GORME

Outstanding singers—and storytellers. They spend a great deal of their time on the road, but our show is home when they are in town. New vocalists rise and fall, but they remain solid. Talent may have something to do with that.

MADELINE KAHN

She's great fun. She's completely off the wall. There's no way of knowing in what direction she'll go. But you can be sure there'll be a funny finish. Every now and then she proves she's an accomplished singer. We'd like her more often than we get her.

GEORGE BURNS

What can you say? He's just plain sensational. He's ninety-one years old, chock-full of show-business stories, ready to do two obscure songs and make them sound like classics. Hurry back, George.

MARIETTE HARTLEY

Another attractive actress who doesn't take herself too seriously. She's smart enough to poke fun at herself and make the audience identify with her. Welcome aboard.

BOB UECKER

A self-proclaimed failure as a big-league baseball catcher, but he's turned his ineptitude into a major-league show-business success. He's not liable to become a Baseball Hall of Famer, but his deadpan delivery and his commercials have made his appearances a comedic home run.

JACK LEMMON

I would venture that he is the most universally respected and admired individual and actor in the business. An ardent supporter of all the "good" causes, he's a star in every sense of the word. He's also a much better than average pianist, but he will play only if you ask him.

DABNEY COLEMAN

First rate and funny. Always sparks Carson and clearly has a good time himself.

HARVEY KORMAN AND TIM CONWAY

Premiere second bananas. They're great contributors individually but even better in tandem. Both devote a good deal of their time to sponsoring charity drives for unfortunate children, as well as to making people laugh.

BOB NEWHART

Originally an accountant, he brings that conservative and double-breasted image to his comedy routines. He and Johnny have great fondness for each other, and we are delighted when his series activities make him available to us. His closest friend, Don Rickles (a longtime *Tonight Show* regular), and he are opposite sides of the coin, on stage and off. Their combined home movies and their experiences while traveling together are hilarious. The Rickleses, the Newharts, and the de Cordovas often vacation together. They make that ten days worth waiting for. All year long.

ROGER MOORE, MICHAEL CAINE, DUDLEY MOORE, AND SEAN CONNERY

Each member of the suave Overseas Quartet is an expert storyteller. All are audience favorites, but, unfortunately, they agree to come abroad only when they have a picture to plug. Fortunately, they work often. And we're glad they do.

BURT REYNOLDS

Mr. Superstar. He's the first to admit that *The Tonight Show* was a major springboard for his success. His self-mocking sense of humor makes him a delight to our audiences. Deep down he'd love to be Johnny. And Johnny would love to be Burt.

JOAN COLLINS, LONI ANDERSON, DYAN CANNON, ALI MACGRAW, CANDICE BERGEN, VICTORIA PRINCIPAL, LINDA EVANS, CYBILL SHEPHERD

The turn-ons. Each is beautiful and an accomplished conversationalist. They have worked at their craft and are respected actresses, as well as beauties.

TERESA GANZEL AND VICTORIA JACKSON
 Two daffies. Attractive and really off the wall. Good actresses and genuinely funny talkers.

SAMMY DAVIS, JR., ALAN KING, GEORGE SEGAL, DAVID STEINBERG, STEVE LANDESBERG, GEORGE CARLIN, JOE GARAGIOLA, MARTIN MULL, DOM DELUISE, ROBERT KLEIN
 All "for sure" pleasing visitors to our couch, and each knows how much we await his availability.

LUCIANO PAVAROTTI, PLACIDO DOMINGO, JUDITH BLEGEN, MARILYN HORNE, MARTINA ARROYO, JULIA MIGENES-JOHNSON, CAROL NEBLETT, BEVERLY SILLS
 Our opera stable. Johnny's ability to make them people rather than visitors from a different planet pleases them and us and our viewers.

LINDA RONSTADT, MELISSA MANCHESTER, CYNDI LAUPER, BARRY MANILOW, DIANA ROSS, TONY BENNETT, JULIO IGLESIAS, DOLLY PARTON, WILLIE NELSON, GLEN CAMPBELL, MAC DAVIS, RAY CHARLES, BELINDA CARLISLE
 They all make music a pleasure.

(To the reader): A *Tonight Show* distinction is that all our performers are required to work live—no lip synch, no click tracks—so we feel that it's a tribute to Doc and the band and our sound technicians that these stars will join us (when their albums are about to be released) and have confidence that we will present them without scarring their images.

BILL COSBY

Even when he wasn't the enormous hit he is today, he was nice and funny and special. He deserves all the success he's having—again.

ROBERT BLAKE

The ultimate rebel. About three times a year he uses our program as a forum to explain the mistakes he's made in his private life and his career and to emphasize the disdain he feels for the network executives he is forced to work with. At the same time, he carefully plugs his upcoming movies or TV programs.

CHARLES GRODIN

One of the many "I-know-his-face-but-not-his-name" first-class actors who play antagonist roles with Johnny. Each appearance is a happy one.

and

THE CLASSICAL MUSICIANS

Horacio Gutierrez, Nadja Salerno-Sonnenberg, Itzhak Perlman, YoYo Ma

and

THE OUTSTANDING JAZZ MUSICIANS AND VOCALISTS

B. B. King, Joe Williams, Pete Fountain, and Dizzy Gillespie

and

THE ALWAYS AMUSING SPORTS FIGURES

Golf's Lee Trevino and Jan Stephenson
Basketball's Magic Johnson and Jerry West
Baseball's Tommy Lasorda and Steve Garvey
Football's Joe Theisman and Jim McMahon
Auto Racing's Danny Sullivan
Tennis's Martina Navratilova and Jimmy Connors

and

THE YOUNG COMEDIANS

Our pride and joy. The crop changes as they move upward and onward, but for now

Louie Anderson, Steven Wright, Kevin Nealon, Gary Shandling, Jay Leno, Jerry Seinfeld, Roseanne Barr

and

THE AT-ONE-TIME-YOUNG COMEDIANS

Who have established themselves and made the big breakthrough and who, happily, remember the old days and return to us every now and then

Richard Pryor, Eddie Murphy, Robin Williams, Buddy Hackett, Rodney Dangerfield, Albert Brooks, Steve Martin

Those are some of the names we look forward to having with us. There are quite a few who, sad to say, aren't quite so welcome. But why speak rudely about the living?

PART TWO

Johnny
and Me

Fred Who?

It is possible that those of you who have read this far may have asked yourself from time to time: Just who the hell does this Fred guy think he is? What qualifies him to make all these judgment calls? What makes him such an authority? I think it's time to fill you in. Then we'll get back to Johnny and *The Tonight Show*.

Looking back, it's difficult to pinpoint just when and where it all started to go right. And what was the true basis for all these eventful years.

It might have been because my father, who was one of our country's most successful "confidence men," loved the bright lights and the bright people and began taking me to theaters and sporting events from the time I was eight. Not too many youngsters attended the opening night of a *Ziegfeld Follies* and saw a cowboy named Will Rogers spin a rope, chew gum, and tell jokes—all at the same time. Or went to the old, old, old Madison Square Garden (way back when it was situated, oddly enough, in Madison Square) and saw Benny Leonard defend his lightweight title against southpaw Lew Tendler. But I was there for those and lots of other "special events." And I found them exciting—and I still do.

Or it might have been because my mother went to a Catholic grade school in New York City with Catherine Dealy, who eventually married J.J. Shubert (one-half of the famous, or infamous, "Shuberts," who owned just about every legitimate theater in the nation) and was the mother of John Shubert, with whom I went to Harvard Law School and who suggested that I might find show business more fun than the law. I thought he was right, and in 1933 I became Johnny Shubert's assistant, with a desk just outside his office on the fifth floor of the Sardi Building on West Forty-fourth Street, at a salary of twenty-five dollars a week to start. That was, of course, just a temporary salary. In slightly over a year my superior talents were recognized and I was upped to thirty dollars a week.

Whether it was because of my mother or my dad, I have been exposed, pleasantly most of the time, to almost every theatrical, political, sports, and front-page luminary for the past sixty-five years. And I still am, up to and including last night's *Tonight Show*.

Most of you who know my name at all probably associate it with my occupation since October 11, 1970 —my starting date as producer of the Johnny Carson program. Johnny first appeared as the host of *Tonight* in 1962 and employed four producers before I hove into view.

Those seventeen years comprise 884 weeks, 4,220 programs, and 14,470 guests . . . so far. Most of my memories of those years are extremely pleasant ones, although not every guest was an absolute doll and not every show rated a place in a time capsule. Some of our guest hosts posed some problems, and on one or two occasions Mr. Carson was less than my most ardent admirer.

Perhaps I should point out that I didn't exactly stumble in from the raisin groves of Fresno and roll accidently into *The Tonight Show*'s producer's office. Long before, I had managed to associate myself with some remarkably talented stars and some equally outstanding programs in the world of television (we'll get to motion pictures and the Broadway stage a little down the line).

In 1953, '54, and '55 I produced and directed the Burns and Allen shows. Gracie was as lovely to work with as she appeared to be addle-pated on the tube. She really was one of a kind. George Burns was, and is, a dear friend—and the first to admit that he is very tough to work with. He knows exactly how his written material should appear on the air and he has always had enormous faith in his head writer—George Burns. I didn't always agree with him, and, in all fairness, he didn't change his mind. I love him a lot now . . . but there were moments!

I had seven super years as producer/director of *The Jack Benny Program* and a bundle of his Specials. When people say "He was in a class by himself," they are talking about Jack. He was the best editor of material and the true master of timing. And, in direct opposition to the character he portrayed, the most generous man in the world. He and his wife (Mary Livingston Benny) and I and my wife spent as many nights together socially as I spent days with him on the set. Those are days and nights I miss—a lot.

For two seasons I was assigned by CBS to oversee Ida Lupino and Howard Duff during what turned out to be seventy-eight tense and martini-filled weeks during the making of *Mr. Adams and Eve*. It was, in my opinion, which I respect, the first sophisticated situation comedy to arrive on television. But very few of the comedic scripts were as convoluted as were the problems in getting the day's work done. After two

Jack Benny, Dennis Day (top), Rochester (top right), Don Wilson (bottom left) and a much younger F de C (bottom right)—plus "The Entire Benny Program Staff."

George Burns, Gracie Allen and I celebrate the end of a happy season on TV.

Acting with Ida Lupino was fun. Directing her was fun too—sometimes.

years I requested a permanent leave of absence. Everyone voted in favor of the motion.

Five years went quickly by while I directed, and often produced as well, the extremely successful *December Bride*. The darling Spring Byington, Harry Morgan (pre-*M*A*S*H*), and a remarkable group of underrated character actors and actresses proved, week after week, that the geriatric picture need not be a gloomy one.

Dick and Tommy Smothers have often been pictured as "strange." And indeed they are. I replaced a harried producer/director on their first series, in which Tommy played an angel. My predecessor fled the scene, totally unable to cope with the Smothers brand of zaniness—on and off screen. I quickly learned to understand his reaction but found their brand of humor and their resentment of restraint almost fun to cope with and was sure they would go on to great success. They did, as you know, and, at their peak, that same resentment of restraint did them in. Time has mellowed them a tad, and I'm always pleased when they show up on *The Tonight Show*.

As challenging as anything I've ever done were my three years directing my golfing buddies Fred Mac-Murray and the late Bill Demarest in the enormously successful *My Three Sons*. The Devil himself must have negotiated Fred's contract with the producer, Don Fedderson. Try this on: thirty-nine episodes, five days needed to shoot each episode—a total of 195 workdays. Fred appeared in almost every scene but was required to show up for only fifty-five days. A production magician (John Stephens, now the head honcho on the very successful *Simon & Simon*) figured out a jigsaw-puzzle format and said it was feasible. It turned out to be—but, even after the fact, I still don't think it can be done. Unfortunately, all those days off didn't help MacMurray's golf swing.

Besides the programs I've mentioned, I enjoyed some unforgettable highs—directing the first Bing Crosby TV Special, starring Bing and Jack Benny and, according to the censors, a too-explicit dance by Sheree North. It was a first-class sixty minutes and described by some critics as "years before its time." I've almost convinced myself that was a compliment.

And there was an incredible four-week period directing Noël Coward, Claudette Colbert, and Betty Bacall "live" in Coward's own stage success *Blithe Spirit*. There were daily problems during rehearsals, and one of life's never-to-be-forgotten moments happened as I was standing only two feet away from Miss Colbert, who, in response to an unnecessarily rude remark from Mr. Coward, swung from the hip and knocked the Dean of Sophisticated English Comedy onto his smart-ass ass.

Betwixt and between, I busied myself by shepherding a few more productions that went on to success. There was the pilot episode starring Bob Cummings as a sexually oriented photographer in the shrewdly named *Bob Cummings Show*. And *When in Rome,* featuring John Forsythe, who has become slightly better known as Blake Carrington in *Dynasty*. And I was delighted when asked to step in as Elizabeth Montgomery made nose-twitching a national pastime in *Bewitched*. You may be sure I was never late to work when directing Inger Stevens in *The Farmer's Daughter*.

When time permitted, I managed to guide Donna Reed as the perfect wife in a number of her programs, and found Gene Barry both talented and congenial (although that may not be a majority opinion), après-*Bat Masterson* and pre-*La Cage aux Folles*, in *Burke's Law*. And overtime didn't upset me while doing *The Doris Day Show*.

During those television days, and completely apart

Elvis and I with the staff of *Frankie and Johnny*. What a nice young man he was!

Jack Benny, Bing Crosby and guess who! I directed Bing's first TV special.

from my movie-studio days, I managed to sneak in enough time to direct two full-sized and acceptably successful motion pictures. One—*I'll Take Sweden*—starred the truly remarkable Bob Hope plus Tuesday Weld, Frankie Avalon, and Dina Merrill. The second, *Frankie and Johnny,* put me together with the most polite and gentlemanly young man I've ever met—Elvis Presley. I got to know him well—in the days before the image cracked—and I'll always be pleased about that.

Finally, since this is a justification of my hiring as Carson's producer, I feel obliged to point out that I wasn't just another journeyman producer/director. Bill Dozier, the boss of Columbia Studios, once engaged me to oversee their television operations, at a decent salary plus some perks and privileges. Unfortunately, while my investiture was widely heralded, my tenure was extremely brief. Before my carefully selected desks and sofas were delivered to my office I was no longer a member of the management team. Nor was Mr. Dozier. He was terminated and guess who was invited to accompany him out? But I feel that even two weeks in charge of a major studio deserves a place in a résumé.

If that episode indicates that the higher-ups in show business are inclined to act in a truth-is-stranger-than-life fashion, please continue for another page or two.

Recently—actually, at a reception for George Burns's ninetieth birthday—I ran into the extremely attractive singer/actress Diahann Carroll, who reminded me of our first meeting. I didn't need a reminder: I'll never forget the most bizarre directing job I've ever had.

The Top Brass at CBS initiated a very hush-hush, high-priority project involving Freeman Gosden and Charlie Correll, who had been the most successful comedy team in the history of radio—Amos and

Andy. Years later they were heavy stockholders in CBS and decided they were interested in appearing as themselves *and* as Amos and Andy in a television series. Everyone at the top was enchanted.

I was selected to direct. It was stressed that the project was to be kept under wraps—no publicity *at all*. We addressed ourselves to solving a major technical problem: how to enable Correll and Gosden to appear as their Caucasian selves, cross to another area of the stage, and arrive there as the black-faced Amos and Andy. I have no idea how the technicians managed to make magic, but they did.

Next, I convinced my friend James Mason to portray a historian of black comedy and engaged two wonderful dancers—Geoffrey Holder and Carmen de Lavallade—and a lovely and talented young singer, Diahann Carroll.

I taped the show on a "closed set," put it together, looked at it carefully, and knew it was all I had hoped for—and more. It was private-pouched to New York —the Brass said it was first-rate and would be shown to "the boys" the next night.

Two days later I was sent for. Behind closed doors I was handed an unexpected and more-than-generous bonus check and a large mail pouch. The first, it was explained, was for the "truly fine job" I had done on the project; the mailbag contained the one and only copy of the program. Correll and Gosden had seen the tape, thought it was even better than they had hoped, but had decided that the prospect of a television series was more than they could handle "at this time in their lives." I was instructed to take the tape—the sole evidence of the project—proceed to the incinerator, and make sure that every bit of it burned up.

Why? Because the decision to scrap the project was a "purely personal one." The stars had thoroughly enjoyed the experience but not enough to work that hard on a regular basis. They felt it important that nobody should view the tape and assume that they were unhappy with their performances or the show itself.

Two months of intensive care burned in three minutes, and I took a Hawaiian vacation with the bonus money. The Corrells and the Gosdens and the de Cordovas met often during the ensuing years, but the subject of the Amos and Andy Special was never mentioned. One more piece of the puzzle: Some six months after I returned from Hawaii, I received a 12″ × 16″ Tiffany silver frame engraved:

To Our Favorite Director, from
Freeman and Charlie

Several of my friends have seen the frame and asked me to explain the inscription. I can't—and it's possible that only Shirley MacLaine can.

On that note it may be necessary to move on and upward to my motion-picture "achievements"—the pictures that turned me into something less than a household name. But it is time for us to return to Johnny's office. And he doesn't like to be kept waiting.

Step by Step
(Continued)

We are back in J.C.'s office. He displays considerable lack of enthusiasm for the mélange we have organized for tonight's entertainment, but stops short of physical punishment. Instead he decides to do a little testing: Have we heard of, for instance, a young English singing star Paul Young? Yes, we have, he's in London at the moment, but his American agent says he'll probably be with us in a month or two. Next question, please. Is there any particular reason that Paul Newman does a lot of other shows but is never booked by us? Indeed there is. Paul isn't "into" small talk about his upcoming movie, he is primarily interested in furthering the success of the Scott Newman Foundation, formed to combat drug abuse among the young. Clearly that's a most worthy cause but is a more likely subject for *Sixty Minutes* or *The Donahue Show* than for our assortment of comedians, vocalists, and bimbos. Before the probing goes further, Mr. Quinn, our director, and Mr. Siller, our head writer, knock on the door and join us.

Siller is informed that the comedy spot may have

been amusing to him and his colleagues but is less than a triumph with Mr. C. Maybe, Siller says, it can be improved and be used tomorrow. The consensus is that it certainly can be improved, but there's doubt it can be improved enough. Remember I predicted we'd be doing "Stump the Band"?

Music-rehearsal time is 3:15, so Bobby and I exit the executive office and move to the stage for the "melody period." We are confident that Doc, the NBC orchestra, and the sound technicians will be organized and ready to start. We are less confident that our scheduled singing star, her backup singers, and her "very own" rhythm section will show up on time. We are correct. For some strange reason, vocalists know exactly how many notes there are to a bar, recognize that thirty-two bars constitute a chorus, but fail to compute the sixty-minutes-make-an-hour equation. Ultimately, they will show up complaining that the traffic since they were last in Los Angeles has become impossible, or that they were unable to find NBC (which has remained in exactly the same spot since 1952), or that their alarm didn't go off. At 3:15 in the afternoon? We have learned to accept that singers operate on DWT—daylight whatever time.

Rehearsal finally starts, the two agreed-upon three-minute songs run a total of nine minutes and "can't possibly be cut." We explain that if that's the case, we'll have to be satisfied with one number only. Somehow the impossible cuts are quickly made. SOP—standard operating procedure.

Doc and the band rehearse a chart, just in case one of our guests doesn't show up or turns out to be a certified nerd who clams up immediately after he makes his entrance. In that case, Johnny will say that we've had numerous requests for a band number and hopes Doc has one ready. Doc will pretend to be surprised but will be ready, and it will sound so truthlike that even Mr. Nerd will never know it is all his fault. We, like the Boy Scouts, are prepared.

It is 4:30, and once again the staff meets in my office for a final brushup. I explain:

1. Johnny will do his monologue.

2. "Stump the Band" will replace the written comedy spot.

3. In the first commercial, Johnny will hold up a box of new, strengthened and fortified detergent.

4. Our first guest will sing her most recent and successful single (which will run three minutes). After applause she will proceed to the chair next to Johnny, stopping only to kiss him on the cheek, bending her right leg behind her while so doing. (That ritual never varies unless the singer happens to be left-legged.)

5. Next commercial and station break.

6. Johnny will talk to the singer. He'll be careful not to ask anything more provocative than "What do you do in your spare time?" or "When you're on the road, do you take your children with you?" Anything heavier than that is liable to be answered with an open mouth and a glazed look. It is time for the second vocal (which will run exactly three minutes).

7. Time for another commercial.

8. Our second guest will be a character actor about to appear in an upcoming movie of the week on "another network," which prohibits us from showing a clip (inter-network warfare continues). He's been with us before and will be both amusing and likable. He and Johnny will enjoy about seven minutes together. So will the audience.

9. Another commercial.

10. The third and final—unless we turn to the band number—guest will most likely be an attractive young actress bountiful of bust and "simply delighted" to meet Johnny Carson. Hopefully, she will flirt a little, display a slightly bawdy sense of humor, and finally

mention that she likes Johnny because she has always been attracted to "older men." The audience will howl at Johnny's injured expression.

11. Final commercial, "thanks" to the guests and the audience, and a promo telling who will be with us the next night.

All that is left to do, after this office rundown, is the show itself. The chances are that what happens during the telecast will be essentially what we have indicated.

At 5:20 I greet the audience, tell them a few jokes, introduce Doc, who will lead the band in a short number, then introduce Ed, who will do a proven four-minute warm-up.

A hush will fall over the audience of five hundred, I'll cue the band, they'll start *The Tonight Show* theme, and Ed will intone, "And now . . . heeeeere's Johnny!" Johnny will come through the center of the monologue curtain, the applause will be long and loud . . . and one hour later, air time, sixteen million people will turn out their lights and call it a day.

Not so Carson, de Cordova, Lassally, McCawley, and Quinn. We will meet, one more time, in Johnny's office and perform an autopsy on the body of the show. It is a clinical, controlled evaluation of exactly what happened. Oddly enough, chances are we'll agree with Mr. Carson's thoughts on the subject. It is likely he will be both perceptive and accurate. In addition, we remember who signs the checks.

Finally, it is time to go home, find out that the air conditioner cannot be repaired, the warranty has, indeed, run out, and the new units have been ordered and will be installed "as soon as possible." That guarantees that we are in for a heat wave.

The <u>Tonight</u> <u>Show</u>
Starring Johnny Carson
... Sometimes

Johnny Carson has hosted *The Tonight Show* for twenty-five years. But you may have noticed that from time to time his chair has been occupied by someone else. Johnny's contracts have allowed him considerable time off—to relax and at the same time recharge his energy batteries. And understandably so. I'm sure you've heard that "the show must go on," and it can't do that unless someone sits behind that famous desk and asks a number of guests a number of provocative questions.

Not too many people, I have learned, are both equipped and available to function acceptably in a role that is much more intricate and demanding than it appears. Movie and television and sports stars, given that they may be articulate and charming and humorous, have their own demanding schedules. And those who *do* have plenty of time on their hands deserve it.

We have tried, with varying results, just about everyone we could think of as a replacement. Most of them have found the experience "fascinating," "beyond belief," "the ultimate dream"; a few have found it "frightening"; and one or two have indicated to me that there isn't enough money in the world for them to do it again.

Some of our guest hosts have been singers who felt that this was the perfect opportunity to be funny—and weren't. Some comedians have used the chair to show that they are serious and profound—and shouldn't have. Many have learned that their bag of tricks was empty after a surprisingly short space of time. And some, thank God, have been just great.

As a reader and as a writer, I am aware that lists can quickly put you to sleep; but please stay awake long enough to scan the variety of names and talents and personalities of some of "Johnny's guest host tonight is":

Joey Bishop	Rob Reiner
Jerry Lewis	Beverly Sills
Roy Clark	Barbara Mandrell
John Davidson	Steve Allen
Kirk Douglas	Robert Blake
Robert Goulet	Bert Convy
Shecky Greene	John Denver
Fernando Lamas	Lola Falana
Rich Little	Burt Bacharach
Chevy Chase	Robert Klein
Helen Reddy	Michael Landon
Debbie Reynolds	Don Meredith
Don Rickles	Jay Leno
McLean Stevenson	Della Reese
Shelley Winters	Charles Nelson Reilly
Sammy Davis, Jr.	George Segal
Kermit the Frog	Barbara Walters
Billy Crystal	Richard Benjamin
Roger Moore	Richard Dawson

Alan King	Bob Newhart
Patrick Duffy	Freddie Prinze
Martin Mull	Burt Reynolds
Kenny Rogers	Tony Danza
Frank Sinatra	Smothers Brothers
Garry Shandling	Orson Welles
David Brenner	George Carlin
Glen Campbell	Gabriel Kaplan
Bill Cosby	Harvey Korman
Dom DeLuise	Steve Martin
Ernie Ford	Vincent Price
Arnold Palmer	Diana Ross
Jack Klugman	Dick Cavett
Steve Lawrence	David Steinberg

Still awake? Deeply concerned that there are two names missing from the list? Not to worry, I'll get to David Letterman and Joan Rivers shortly.

But first I should point out that neither Ed McMahon nor Doc Severinsen has ever hosted the program—by their own choice. Several times Johnny has suggested that I turn to them when we faced an emergency replacement problem, and both declined politely but firmly. Doc and Ed star on their own in many venues, but on *The Tonight Show* they prefer to remain Johnny's musical conductor and sidekick. I'm glad—they have been towers of strength on a number of occasions when some of our guest hosts have found themselves adrift and in danger of sinking.

Along the way, the show has struck gold in the substitute-host area a number of times. Even when his career wasn't as sparkling as it is now, Bill Cosby combined humor and charm and inventiveness. He made it fun for all of us.

So too did Burt Reynolds. Audiences loved his self-

Jack Albertson handing me an Emmy.

The Five Musketeers: Doc, Bobby, Johnny, Fred, Ed.

deprecating style, even before, and certainly after, the *Cosmopolitan* centerfold. But Bill and Burt's immense success diminished their availability to us. Several for whom we had high hopes didn't live up to them; several were good but not good enough; but for most it was a "sometime thing," and we were searching for an "often thing."

The Tonight Show didn't discover David Letterman. But it was "there" and he was "there" at the proper time, and it was good for both. David was a guest many times and our audiences loved him. He hosted the show often, and the format fit him like a glove. It was obvious that before long he'd have his own show. He got it—and it wasn't a hit. He got another show—and that didn't work, either. When the time slot following Carson opened up, both Johnny and NBC felt he was made to order for it. Now *Late Night with David Letterman* is an enormous success, and everyone who knows him is delighted.

It's strange that two major figures in late-night television are so outgoing and garrulous on the air, so completely at home before a camera and an audience of strangers, and, at the same time, so shy and private in their personal lives. David even more than Johnny. Letterman truly hates social gatherings, fashionable restaurants, and shirts and ties. He enjoys a small circle of close friends, beach life, and remains in awe of Carson. All three traits are shared by Johnny.

For some time the media have made attempts to create a feud between Letterman and Carson. I'm not sure which of them considers it more absurd. You can take it from me, insider-wise, that no one is more pleased than J.C. about D.L.'s success, and no one is less eager than D.L. to move into J.C.'s time slot.

Each of them is happy where he is. I use the initials D.L and J.C. to protect myself in case my evaluation should prove to be faulty.

So, Johnny has his own show, David has his own show, and, as you may have heard, so did Joan Rivers.

Joan Rivers

For three years Joan was the one and only guest host of *The Tonight Show*—behind that desk for eight weeks and forty shows, scheduled to appear once every six weeks or so. She was very talented, very funny, very successful—and very controversial. In October of 1986 she opted for an adversarial position. Many people felt she would be a strong opponent when she went head to head against us on the air. Many people felt the same way when Johnny was challenged by Dick Cavett, Merv Griffin, Mike Douglas, Joey Bishop, Sammy Davis, Jr., Jerry Lewis, John Barbour, Jack Paar (yes, he made a comeback attempt), and Allan Thicke, among others. Recently millions of viewers had the opportunity to make the choice—Johnny or Joan. And one more time the decision was made. Joan joined the parade of those who fired and fell back.

It is unlikely that any television personality, including Howard Cosell, has inspired more protest mail than Miss Rivers. Our staff keeps a record of all the mail the program receives: the number of requests for autographed photos, gifts for Johnny, suggestions for guest appearances, cartoons and jokes, cassettes of "talented" friends and acquaintances, and pro and con comments on our guests and guest hosts. The letters on Joan always ran twenty to one—against.

In all fairness, she has provoked consistent hostility, when she was merely making jokes. People protested when Joan said:

• Elizabeth Taylor was so fat they had to grease her thighs to shove her through the Golden Arches at McDonald's.

• English animal lovers were up in arms at being told that Princess Margaret looks like a horse.

• airline stewardesses keep reaching for the overhead compartments to prove to male passengers they aren't wearing panties.

• hospital nurses can't wait for patients to be taken to surgery so they can short-sheet their beds.

• she'd invite Joan Collins to discuss the men she'd been with, but the program only runs for an hour.

• Marie Osmond is such a goody-goody that the Pope wired her to "loosen up."

• it's okay to call Sophia Loren a tramp, because she doesn't know who I am anyway.

• most wives are so unsexy that when their husbands say "Roll over," they know they are talking to their dog.

• and God didn't mean Jewish people to exercise and bend over, or He'd have put diamonds on the floor.

In general, Joan managed to irritate a wide cross section of the viewing public, even when she poked fun at herself, her own figure, and her (very happy) married life with Edgar. The public, apparently, laughed at what she said but resented her at the same time. Her ratings were very good (not as good as she claimed) when she operated under *The Tonight*

Show's umbrella and under a rigid system of supervision as to guests and the acceptable limits of taste. But when she and Edgar took the operation into their own hands, an unhappy ending seemed a foregone conclusion. Someone should have pointed out that being "against Johnny" was a far different world from "sitting in" for him.

When she moved on, the press, with Joan's help, tried to make it seem as if a state of war existed between her show and ours. That was never the case. Each year there's another group of hopefuls who enter the late-night arena. This year it was Joan . . . and David Brenner and Dick Cavett and Jimmy Breslin and Dick Clark. They are all entitled to make a run at us, and maybe someday one of them will succeed.

In all candor, Johnny was rather ticked off at Joan, but only at the manner in which she announced her departure. A second-hand discovery that a member of your family has moved out of your home doesn't make for joy and celebration. I enjoyed working with Joan, but her manner of saying bye-bye to Johnny and *The Tonight Show* was, in my opinion, somewhere between tacky and tasteless. If Joan were to tell the truth, I think she would have to agree.

But telling the truth is not necessarily the number-one priority in the Rivers world. Joan appears to enjoy creating a crisis and then expressing wide-eyed surprise at what has happened. She will then arrange, through her very active press agent, to be wounded and/or betrayed at the self-created turn of events. A lot of time and trouble could be saved if "just the facts, ma'am" fit into her lifestyle.

You'd like some specific examples? You got 'em.

The Patti Davis Cancellation

For instance, on March 5, 1986, Joan, as guest host, signed off the telecast by billboarding her guests for "tomorrow night." She announced them as: "Peter Allen, Valerie Harper, comedian Arsenio Hall, *and* . . . daughter of the Ronald Reagans, Patti Davis."

At 10:15 on March 6, 1986, my first phone call of the day was from Joan (with Edgar on an extension) explaining: "This is what you have to do for me, Fred." I was, quite simply, to cancel Patti Davis's appearance on the show *that* night. I was to explain that Joan had just finished Patti's book and, as a wife and mother, couldn't handle the interview. "Actually, Fred, and you mustn't breathe a word of this, I have received a call from Washington asking me to cancel Patti." Whether this was actually the case or Joan was merely worried about offending "Washington," I didn't and don't know, but I explained that the media would be on us like a plague and that *The Tonight Show* had never canceled a guest under circumstances like these and didn't function in that fashion. I even offered to call the White House and explain the problem that was about to ensue. "No, please, don't do that. It would do more harm than good." I finally agreed to call Patti's publisher and tell her that the booking was canceled but that *The Tonight Show* would "make no explanation." I told Joan: "This is your problem and your press people will have to make any statements." Joan and Edgar said "We'll take care of everything" but I should hurry and cancel Patti and then book a replacement right away. I did.

The story broke as if it were truly front-page news. My phones rang continuously. I arranged for a standard answer: Miss Davis would not be appearing on the program; any further comment would have to come from Richard Grant, Miss Rivers's press agent. Mr. Grant, when phoned by the wire services, threw the following curve: "Miss Rivers does not book the guests on *The Tonight Show*. Maybe for some reason NBC is trying to pass the buck." I finally decided that the truth should be told and gave a statement to the press:

> The show's staff does not book anybody who is not suggested by the host or hostess, or is not discussed in advance with the host or hostess. There are no surprise bookings.

I added that:

> I've known Miss Davis for a long time and would not want her to think I initiated the events. She is a friend and so are her parents.

As a final note in this saga, I must point out that Miss Rivers had *insisted* on the Davis booking in the first place in spite of my rather lukewarm reaction. I *had* read the book.

The facts are equally clear on Joan's move to star in her own show. She was certainly entitled to do so. She's a distinct talent, and under different circumstances, we'd all have wished her the best of luck. Everyone knows that show business is a cutthroat world, success is transitory, and dog is entitled to eat dog. But . . .

Early in March, Johnny decided to continue for another year. His contract entitled him to end his deal with NBC on September 7, 1986, if he so decided. As soon as he said he was going to extend for another year, he asked me (a) if Joan would go along, and (b) if her "figures" had held up acceptably. I said they had and that I thought she'd be pleased to continue. He told Henry Bushkin, his lawyer, to inform NBC to open negotiations. They did. Everyone expected she'd ask for more money and that she was entitled to it—within reason.

NBC reported back in mid-April that Joan's negotiators were difficult to reach, hard to pin down, and didn't return their calls. Joan appeared as a guest on the show with Johnny on April 25 and later claimed she "almost" told him that night that she was finalizing a deal with Fox. But she didn't. The next week she hosted the show for five days; I spent six hours a day with her discussing her monologues and possible guests for the upcoming weeks she was scheduled to host our show. She never mentioned directly, or even by innuendo, that she was discussing an outside deal. Her manager, Bill Sammeth, did, in fact, ask me when our schedule would be "firmed for next year" so Joan's Vegas dates could be arranged around it.

Monday, May 5, 1986, Joan (and Edgar on extension) called me at home at 7:00 P.M. Tearfully, she had "something to tell me": she had made a deal with Fox to do a talk show. It would start in October. It would be on the air opposite Johnny. She was calling me first and would shortly call and tell Johnny and Peter Lassally, in that order. I was stunned. All I could say to Joan was, "You're kidding." She told me how dear I was to her—Edgar said the deal was for three years and there would "always be a candle in the window" for me. I repeated, "You're kidding!" Then I called Johnny immediately. He had just received a call from NBC boss Brandon Tartikoff telling him that Joan had, indeed, made a deal with Fox and a press conference was scheduled by her for the next day. While John and I were talking, he was told that Joan was on his other phone. He said he wouldn't take the call—it was "a little late in arriving . . . about three months late."

I phoned Peter, who wasn't home. The next morning Joan reached Peter and offered him a three-year deal as producer of her show—"firm, and don't worry about the money." Later she denied that such an offer was ever made. Or that offers were made to every one of our coordinators, each of whom said no and gave me the details of their offers.

The day she held the press conference, she and Fox declared that she would be doing *The Joan Rivers Show*, starting in October, from eleven till twelve, that she couldn't understand Carson's attitude, and that she had to do what she had to do. After all, she explained, her ratings were higher than those of "the current host" (not true), her rate card—commercial price—was higher than Johnny's (*also not true*), and now she'd be free to book the guests she wanted without all the restrictions imposed on her by *The Tonight Show*. The three years she spent with us must have been dismal ones for her.

How Did the Show Go, Dear?

As you slide between the covers at night, most of you know if it was a good day or a lousy day at the office, if your children behaved as you hoped they would, if all the appliances made the housework a piece of cake, or if it rained immediately after your car was washed. And you know you did your best and that's all a person can do. It isn't that simple for me and my cohorts. We appear before a number of juries.

The first group of decision makers—five hundred strong—wait in line for up to five hours before being ushered into Studio One, where they immediately scramble for the best seats. That objective gained, it is likely that they all will then say to themselves or their companions: "This place sure looks smaller than it does on television." All five hundred then turn themselves into instant critics and decide that what is presented to them for their entertainment is the best show they've ever seen or something considerably less. One thing is for sure: if a camera is ever turned in their direction, eighty percent of the audience, no matter what age group they fall into, will wave their arms wildly, make funny faces, and yell out such brilliant comments as "Pittsburgh," "Hook 'em horns," or "Hello, Harry."

Millions of viewers will be watching and evaluating our efforts in the comfort of their beds, but the five hundred in our studio are the only ones we see and hear.

Johnny's monologue is the pride and joy of the program. It has been hailed as the most outstanding comedy-oriented editorial on political events since the days of Will Rogers. Johnny's thrusts at the foibles of government and in-the-news personalities are not only funny; they can focus public attention on a situation in a way the papers and the newscasts can't. *The Wall Street Journal* and *The New York Times* often quote his quips; but that doesn't guarantee that more than five percent of our studio audience has the foggiest notion who or what he is talking about. They can laugh at alimony jokes, the jibes at Dr. Ruth Westheimer, and "it-was-so-hot-today" routines; but the more sophisticated humor may not be so successful. The nights when our audience is composed of knowledgeable people, the program really gets off to a flying start.

Many say that Johnny is at his best when his jokes bomb, and certainly he has a remarkable talent for comic recovery; but while swimming upstream is just fine for salmon—it's not so much so for comedians.

It is unlikely that we've ever thought of a show as one of our best when the monologue went "down the toilet." Also not so desirable is a comedy sketch or a desk piece that doesn't tickle the fancy of the folks out front. On many occasions Johnny will carry on bravely, adding instant humor to what has been written for him; and some of the most hilarious moments result when he knows that what's still to come isn't any funnier than what's already flopped. A dozen or so times when he's decided instant death is better than a lingering comedic illness, he's given me the "that's-it" look, informed the audience that they were right, what he had been doing wasn't funny, and he'd be damned if he was going on with it. He has set fire to the remaining pages of "funny stuff" and deposited them in a wastebasket while Doc played "Taps" on his trumpet. He has also decided in the middle of a sketch that he's gone about as far as he can go, saluted the audience, and said, "This seems to be the perfect time to go to a commercial."

Whenever those things happen—and we wish they didn't—the audiences invariably break out into laughter and applause. They weren't crazy about what he was doing, but they love Johnny and want him to know it.

There are also the programs when the guests cause the problem. The late Orson Welles, a magician in addition to all his other talents, once attempted an intricate mathematical trick. He wrote a six-digit number on a blackboard and concealed it from the cameras and the audience. He then asked four people to shout out five-digit numbers; he added those numbers, uncovered the blackboard, and disclosed that his concealed number was the correct total. Only this night it wasn't even close. He went through the entire process again—and again his answer was wrong. We had wasted twenty minutes and we couldn't explain, of course, that the fourth "shouter" in the audience was a "plant" who knew in advance the number that Orson had originally written, and was supposed to total the numbers yelled out by the others and supply (by use of a calculator) the missing figure. Orson would then have done the impossible! On this occasion he should have chosen an accomplice with a talent for figures, rather than a young lady with a lovely figure.

John Davidson was so upset with himself when he

forgot the lyrics of his song one memorable night that he kicked an audio monitor and shorted all the electrical equipment in the studio. I couldn't even go to a commercial. We telecast a "Best of Carson" rerun that night.

Another "high spot": Shelley Winters was our opening guest and was her usual amusing and daffy self. Our second guest was a well-known and rascally English leading man, Oliver Reed. During his segment he made a number of female-put-down remarks: "Women are generally boring . . . no one should take them seriously . . . cleaning the home and serving their husbands is their proper role in life." Shelley sneaked back into camera range carrying a tumbler of Scotch whisky and slowly but carefully doused Mr. Reed from head to toe. Commercial!

One more moment of note: Our final guest was a young lady large of bust and empty of head. Johnny commented that she was extremely attractive. She thanked him. He asked if she enjoyed film work. She said she did. Where did she come from? Cleveland. Did she have brothers and sisters? No, she didn't. Was she romantically involved? Kind of. He decided to try a question never used before: "We only have a minute left and I'd like an honest answer. Have you ever read a book?" I called for the good-night theme while she was weighing her answer.

Performers are not responsible for all the foul-ups. Experienced and expert as I am supposed to be, I too have goofed and caused a problem. One of my responsibilities is to time each show properly—to leave enough but not too much time for the last guest to sing his song or the comic to complete his routine. When I make a mistake on the short side, Johnny is forced to "fill" or "stretch" even when there's nothing left to talk about. But he can, without much enthusiasm, handle that. If, on the other hand, I don't leave enough time, we are up that very well-known creek. There is, after all, just so much time before we have to sign off and let Letterman come on the air.

B. B. King is a certified jazz great and recently was the closing guest on one of our shows. By my reckoning, his final song would run two and a half minutes and we would fade out on applause. Actually his final number ran *three* and a half minutes, so only the studio audience heard the complete performance. Those at home were surprised to see us disappear from sight in the middle of B.B.'s song.

Mr. Carson explained to me, rather caustically, that even very young children know how to tell time, and it was quite a long while before I could wipe the egg off my face.

Certainly we do some shows that leave something to be desired, but in general we entertain our large and loyal audience. They write and tell us so and we appreciate hearing from them.

And once in a while the mix is great. From start to finish the show is a winner; everything falls into place and the hour seems to take five minutes. The monologue is one big joke after another; the "Mighty Carson Art Players" with Johnny as Rambo or Mr. Reagan or Mr. Rogers or Dr. Ruth is good enough to play on Broadway; and the guests are a delight (maybe it's a combo of Bill Cosby, Placido Domingo, Burt Reynolds; maybe Jimmy Stewart, Dudley Moore, and Itzhak Perlman). It's great fun to shuffle the cards, deal, and come up with an entertainment royal flush.

It happens. Not every night. But when it does it's a pleasure to answer the question: "How did the show go, dear?"

Johnny and Me—
in Private

It was a Monday—that means a rerun for *The Tonight Show*. My booking board showed that we were solidly set for the upcoming week and the writers seemed to know where they were going, so I gave everyone the day off—a holiday for all the staff but me and the receptionist. I needed someone to answer the phone in case the outside world didn't know of my kindness and consideration for my co-workers and I'd be able to clear my desk and be at my post and available if a crisis should arise.

I had just viewed one cassette in which a seven-year-old girl in tuxedo and blackface makeup sang a medley of her favorite Al Jolson hits, and another of a speech expert who, if he were to appear on our show, could show Johnny how to talk more effectively. I wasn't too eager to watch the amusing antics of the Motorcycle Grandmas but would have if I hadn't been saved by the bell: Johnny was in his office and wondered if I was free for lunch. Guess what? I told him (a) that I was much too busy to fit him into my schedule or (b) that I'd be with him in five minutes. I was there in four.

It would be wrong to lead you to believe that Carson had driven all the way from Malibu to Burbank on a nontaping day just to have lunch with Old Friend Fred. Actually there was a good deal of noisy redecorating being done at his home, he was just about to move into his new studio office and wanted to check out all the phones and fixtures, he had a later-in-the-day appointment at the Carson Productions building for an update on his other television projects, and he had forgotten the brown-bag lunch he had intended to bring with him from home. Also, I was the only employee of *The Tonight Show* who was in attendance, except the receptionist, who couldn't leave his designated work area.

At that time NBC was rebuilding and renovating many of its studio buildings, which required moving Johnny from the less-than-sumptuous offices he'd worked out of for fourteen years. They'd relocated him downstairs (into the basement, actually). He agreed to the change but insisted that *his* decorators take charge of the furnishing. As a result, he was about to move into a truly splendid setup, more like a small luxurious apartment than an office.

When I joined him there, he gave me a tour of his newly completed home away from home, and we pronounced that it was fitting and proper for a big star (my words, not his) even if its cellar location made any windows impossible. I pointed out that he could have a simulated window painted on one of the walls. He smiled—a little—and we moved on to other topics of conversation.

On those rare occasions when I've been alone with Johnny and when we aren't together to discuss a specific problem or project, he presents an entirely different personality. Only then does he drop his guard and open himself and his private life to me. Always, however, the conversation is sprinkled with "I'd prefer it if you didn't discuss this with anyone else" or "Let's keep this between ourselves." I've made it a strict rule to observe those confidences, only to find out by accident that Quinn or Bushkin or Lassally is privy to the same information, told to them with the same restriction. That can make for some conversational tap-dancing among us when each of us believes he's the only one who knows how Johnny really feels about something.

On this particular day I got my first indication that Johnny was leaning toward another extension of his contract. NBC had made it clear that they were extremely eager for him to continue doing the show, but he had from time to time expressed doubts that he should. Every now and then he'd ask: "How much longer can we keep doing this?" Or: "You know, our Twenty-fifth Anniversary Show might be the perfect time to pack it in."

He always admitted that he still enjoyed doing the show, that he got "itchy" during his vacation weeks, and that he had no interest in being a movie personality. (He feels strongly that after all his years on the show, motion-picture audiences would never accept him playing a character other than himself.) But, most of all, he didn't want to stay on the air even one second more than the public wanted him to.

This day he mentioned that, contractually, he needed to give the network a yes or no before long. I pointed out that our ratings have never been higher and that in my (totally unsolicited) opinion he would be suicidal two weeks after he decided to call it a day.

He thanked me for my evaluation of him as a well-rounded man of many interests but wrapped up the conversation by saying: "I sure would have a lot of time on my hands, wouldn't I?"

That couldn't be considered a firm commitment but I felt pretty sure I could safely send out my laundry.

Two weeks later Johnny and NBC announced a new two-year deal. My laundryman is happy and so am I.

The most private portion of Johnny's life is his romantic relationships. For several years he has been happily, by every indication, involved with a most attractive lady, Alex Mass, but on the subject of matrimony he often claimed: "I'll get married when the Ayatollah Khomeini is a centerfold in *Playboy*," but this very day he tells me to tell Janet that he and Alex went shopping for an engagement ring. That's good news: Alex is a beauty, has a delightful sense of humor, and seems to be truly dedicated to the happiness of "our boy." Now that he and Alex are married, look for the Ayatollah in *Playboy*.

Quite often in these conversations Johnny will refer, with sadness, to the rather recent deaths of his parents. On the air he reveals little sentimental emotion about anything; but much of his center in life was his warm relationship with his father and mother. His early years, which he refers to as "those childhood days on the plains of Nebraska," were evidently very happy ones, and it's obvious that he misses, constantly, the people who made it so.

I can understand that more than most.

Patience Is a Virtue

It's my guess that by now many of you may be feeling tense and a little uptight. After all, you've been sharing the problems of organizing *The Tonight Show* into the proper shape to go on the air. I know that's a full-time job. And I know there's a lot more you'd like to know about Johnny Carson—the man and the legend. I promise to return to him before too long. But it's only fair to all of us that we continue the de Cordova story and point out that I enjoyed a rather active life long before Mr. Midnight appeared on the scene.

Almost everyone remembers two things: where he or she was when the Japanese attacked Pearl Harbor, and every detail about his or her first sexual encounter. But how many of you remember what you did on the morning of October 2, 1943? Well, I do. I had driven my damn-near-paid-for Ford convertible from Louisville, Kentucky, where I did my summer stint as the producer of the operettas at the Iroquois Amphitheater in that gentle city, to Burbank, California. At 10:00 A.M. I turned into the imposing driveway of the Warner Bros. Studios. I entered the front doors armed with a seven-year contract (with a lot of options, which only they could exercise) and presented myself and my credentials to the security officer at the desk. I explained that I was a former New York stage director, was contractually due to be at the studio that day, and would like to chat with Jack Warner in order to discuss this new facet of my career.

The security officer was very polite. He told me that my name was indeed on the list of Warner employees and that, as a dialogue director, I should report to a Mr. Geller, not Mr. Warner, who would inform me of my duties and responsibilities. But first I should remove my car from the front driveway, proceed to the employees' gate, try to find an open parking place, and be sure I didn't pull into an assigned spot. In my imagined arrival, I had pictured a slightly more impressive reception.

In the Warner Bros. chain of command, the position of dialogue director, I quickly learned, was a considerable number of giant steps below the status of a "real" director. In the dialogue director's mind, however, he was of immense help to the director and far above the assistant director. The assistant director felt, on the other hand, and with some justification, that dialogue directors were primarily stuffy former Broadway stage directors (like me) who knew absolutely nothing about the making of motion pictures and were liable, until they were fired, to hinder, from the day they walked on the set, every attempt to complete, efficiently, the making of a picture.

Possibly they were correct—and, as a matter of fact, the classification of a dialogue director no longer exists. But it was an invaluable stepping-stone for those of us who had had some measure of success in the theater, who were familiar with the spoken word but didn't have idea one about how to film a picture— where to place the camera correctly; what camera lens to use and why; the difference between a fade, a wipe, a dissolve, and a cut. George Cukor, Irving Rapper (Bette Davis's favorite director at Warner's), Vincent Sherman, and I are, or were, prime examples of dialogue directors who moved on to more or less impressive directorial careers and who later always requested that dialogue directors be assigned to their pictures. It would be nice to report that some of the dialogue directors who were, over the years, assigned to me and who learned the basics from me—as I learned them from Michael Curtiz, David Butler, Jean Negulesco, and Irving Rapper—went on to become among the most important directors in the business. It would be nice, but it wouldn't be true. I can't think of a single one who remains in the business. Except me. How come? you ask.

Well, for starters, don't let anyone tell you that sheer talent is the sole criterion for success in show business. I firmly believe that well-tailored suits, the ability to drink martinis without slurring your words, the proper grip on a nine-iron, or on a leading lady while you're dancing, and the restraint not to challenge the obviously stupid remark made by the head of production at your studio—all these are equally important ways to wind up with a good script and an acceptable cast of competent performers. But don't just take my word for it.

The *Motion Picture Almanac* is a widely respected industry authority, published yearly. It is essentially a compendium of the personalities, events, and productions who, and which, have brought taste and talent and success to the movie business. The current edition comprises 667 pages, 297 of which are devoted to a section cleverly titled "Who's Who." There one can find the vital statistics and the filmic accomplishments of the elite of the film world since its inception—if those career greats are still alive. Apparently if you

Deanna Durbin and Fred at Mocambo.

The very special Sonja Henie had my full attention.

die, you are subject to instant erasure. So far I've managed to keep that from happening.

Strangely enough, possibly because I have hung on longer than a large portion of truly contributing talents, there is a rather lengthy list spotlighting the de Cordova motion-picture history.

There is my birthdate, my city of origin, my educational background, my marital status, an all-too-scanty résumé of my Broadway "triumphs," and the following:

PICTURES INCLUDE:

(dialogue director)	*San Antonio*
	Janie
	Between Two Worlds
	Roughly Speaking
	Mildred Pierce
(director)	*Too Young to Know*
	Her Kind of Man
	That Way with Women
	Always Together
	Wallflower
	For the Love of Mary
	Countess of Monte Carlo
	Illegal Entry
	Gal Who Took the West
	Buccaneer's Girl
	Peggy
	The Desert Hawk
	Bedtime for Bonzo
	Katie Did It
	Little Egypt
	Finders Keepers
	Here Come the Nelsons
	Yankee Buccaneer
	Bonzo Goes to College

(director)   *Column South*
                            I'll Take Sweden
                            Frankie and Johnny

While you study that list and determine just which ones belong on your all-time list of Ten Best, you may feel that the works of Billy Wilder or Willie Wyler or George Stevens or Steven Spielberg may be more impressive. You are entitled to your opinion, but keep in mind that I never directed a picture that wasn't a financial success. Let me explain.

During the period I was involved with the above-mentioned films, it was virtually impossible for a studio-produced and studio-released movie to lose money. When a company owned the studio and the theater in which the movie was shown, there wasn't any way but up. Unless, of course, an employee's contract entitled him to a percentage of the profits—creative bookkeeping was invented a long, long time ago.

In spite of my enthusiasm for my work, it is possible that you may not be in complete agreement with my evaluation, but it is equally possible that you may not realize that in my screen classics appeared:

Joan Crawford	Sidney Greenstreet
Rosalind Russell	Humphrey Bogart
John Garfield	Jack Carson
Errol Flynn	Rhonda Fleming
Paul Henreid	Robert Hutton
Bob Hope	Edward Arnold
Jackie Gleason	Robert Benchley
Rock Hudson	Jeff Chandler
Ann Blyth	David Janssen
Joan Leslie	Ethel Barrymore
Sonja Henie	Audie Murphy

Dennis Weaver	Dane Clark
Richard Greene	Faye Emerson
Harry Morgan	Janis Paige
Edmund Gwenn	Diana Lynn
Mark Stephens	S. Z. Sakall
Ozzie and Harriet Nelson	Ronald Reagan

. . . and a host of others, as they say, too numerous to mention, or remember. Many of those named above continued in the business even after being exposed to my directorial touch.

But, false modesty aside, I never made a picture I didn't like . . . until the reviews were printed. Sadly, I liked some of them even after that. The good news is that every now and then I get a letter from some terminal insomniac who saw a picture of mine at 4:00 A.M. and took the time and trouble to say "I enjoyed it." A late-night audience isn't necessarily a stupid audience.

During my directing days I chose to rewrite dozens of scenes to make them, in my opinion, more effective. And I agreed to many performers' requests to alter speeches so that they would feel more comfortable. But I am not a writer in the accepted sense of the word. I wish I were. There must be an enormous sense of satisfaction in facing a blank page and, through one's singular ability, being able to create a character, a scene, and, eventually, a story. And, too, it must be enormously frustrating to watch lesser talents alter and diminish those efforts. Further, by the nature of the motion-picture procedure, only a very small group of writers have had the "muscle" to insure that their words were "written in stone" and cannot be "improved" by unwanted collaborators. This fortunate cadre of elite talents have been able to protect their creations by becoming writer/directors. Orson Welles, Billy Wilder, Woody Allen, Sly Stallone, John Huston, George Stevens, and Joe Mankiewicz have "done it their way," delighted vast audiences, and created great grosses. Other "auteurs" have been less fortunate and have been dehyphenated. Thereby proving that too *few* cooks can also spoil the broth.

While being a writer brings special rewards, so does being a director.

The joys of being a director are many and most rewarding. Assuming one has done one's homework, knows the content and intent of the upcoming day's scenes, has planned the proper camera angles, and has remained on speaking terms with the actors and actresses involved, it is exhilarating to drive through the studio gates, enter the door of "your" sound stage, acknowledge the good-mornings of your crew, point out the camera position for the first shot of the day, and confidently tell the assistant director: "Let's get started."

"Roll 'em," "action," "cut," and "print" have been parodied time and again, but they are basically wonderful words. When a director uses them, at least for that moment the world is his. And, at the end of the day, when the scheduled work has been completed and when, hopefully, all has gone well, there's another thrilling phrase—"that's a wrap"—that belongs to the director alone. It means that it's time for a martini, an evaluation of what has been accomplished, a look at the rushes of the day before—and, of course, it's time to start planning the next day's work.

Certainly there are crosses to bear, as well as delights to savor. These result from the paranoid behavior of some "superstars" a director may have the "luck" to work with. As we all know, actors and actresses are just simple, ordinary folk singled out by God to share their talents with less gifted mortals.

By and large, however, I've had a wonderful time

in the company of this "breed apart." If you can retain your sanity while dealing with them on the set, in their homes, and sometimes in their beds, you've got better than a fifty-fifty chance of enjoying a full and fascinating life. Why don't we chat for a few pages about a few rebels, rogues, romantics, and an actor named Ronald.

Stardust

Almost every commodity on the market is purchased because of its brand name. Cars are from Ford or Chrysler or General Motors; it's Bayer aspirin, Eagle pencils, and Rolex watches. Manufacturers pay a fortune to advertising agencies to come up with a slogan that will identify the product with the company that makes it, and millions are spent to implant that name in the mind of the consumer: "I'll have a Coke"; "Two Duracell batteries, please"; "A. T. and T., the right choice."

Not so in the world of motion pictures. No ticket purchaser really gives a damn if the film is released by MGM or United Artists or Fox or Paramount or Universal. And, except for a very small minority, nobody cares who produced, directed, or wrote it. People go to the movies because of the stars who are in the picture. It was like that when pictures started to move and it's like that now. Even a mediocre effort has a shot if the star is a major one, and good pictures "go through the roof" when combined with superstars. Why else do the Stallones, Allens, Redfords, Streeps, Streisands, and Eastwoods receive such monumental salaries plus a percentage of the net (or even the gross) proceeds?

Not every "name" is, or was, as exciting in private life as on the screen. You can be a crashing bore and still have enormous talent. In my travels through the sound stages, the bistros, and the homes of Hollywood, I've spent some time with the dullards and the sparklers. Let's talk about them with more emphasis on the latter group, starting with Errol Flynn.

The Swashbuckler

During the many days and nights I spent in the company of Errol Flynn, I never received any indication, no matter what you may have read, that he was (a) a Nazi sympathizer or (b) a homosexual. Sexual he certainly was, but homo I doubt very much. And even his distaste for his role as an employee of Jack Warner (one of the original studio owners who felt he also owned all those who worked for him) would hardly have qualified him as a Hitler follower. He was, nonetheless, unusual to work with.

Flynn starred in many western films—most successfully. Each script had to explain his British accent (he was a Tasmanian, actually) by saying that before he landed in Texas, or Missouri, or Kansas, he had spent his youth in Australia. Every screenplay referred to this—by front-office edict—three times, in case the viewer entered the theater after the start of the picture and was confused by this Texan who spoke as if he'd been educated at Oxford.

In these westerns Errol, naturally, rode a horse— usually the same one. It was a beautifully trained, lovely to look at, movie-wise palomino. Flynn invariably requested that he be furnished this particular horse before he agreed to do the picture. Jack Warner, in an uncharacteristic burst of largesse, before we started shooting *San Antonio* called his star to his office, said he understood why Flynn was so attached to the horse and that it would never again be necessary for him to request the palomino. It was now Errol's own horse and "Here is the certificate of ownership." Flynn was truly impressed, embraced Warner, and said how much he appreciated the gesture. He seemed to—till the first day of shooting. On that day he arrived on the set on time—a pleasant surprise—and was asked if he had vanned the horse to the location. Why should he? asked Flynn. After all, his horse was a remarkable animal, highly trained, movie-wise, and no financial deal had been made between him and the studio for its use. He insisted on a very high daily rental and got it. At first Warner was livid at being forced to rent his gift, but once he saw the humor in the situation, he laughed heartily and never forgave Flynn—again.

More on Flynn. As a western star, Flynn was obliged to wear a pistol, of course. It would be drawn by the hero with lightning speed when the script required that the bad man be punished or the virginal leading lady be saved. Very few stars were able to draw faster than Flynn or shoot more accurately. But Flynn saw no reason to go through the film wearing a heavy Colt or Smith & Wesson around his waist when the script called for him to draw it only once or twice. So, except in draw-and-shoot scenes, he wore a light balsa-wood replica of the shooting iron. No problem there except that when his character turned from an embrace with Alexis Smith and faced the cattle rustler, it became the director's problem to intercut the fast draw of the hero with a cut to the bad man drawing his gun, cut back to Flynn as he fired the real gun, cut back to the wounded villain, and finally cut back to Errol as he returned the balsa replica to its holster. Movie magic you never thought of.

More on Flynn. He often took a drink. And followed that drink with another one. And . . . but I'm sure you've got the picture.

Let's travel back to the Bella Union Saloon when it was the best the West had to offer—hundreds of cowpokes bellied up to the bar, its mirror reflecting the scantily clad chorus girls on the stage, the male quartet harmonizing as landowners and prospectors and fancy ladies elbowed their way to the gaming tables. Let's picture all this and realize that these folks are dress extras and stuntmen and bit players awaiting the entrance of Clay Hardin (Mr. Flynn), whose steely eyes will strike terror into the hearts of the unworthy and bring hope to the hearts of the honest men and women that their water rights will be protected. All the while, Alexis Smith and C. Z. Sakall are sure that Clay will never let them down.

But a problem exists. Clay/Flynn is close by. He is, in fact, in his dressing room but won't come out. His director (guess who) has his cameras in their proper positions. The playback music has been rehearsed, the quartet is ready, the dancers are in place. All is prepared—except for one detail. Errol hasn't answered the knock on his door. The second assistant director has failed; the first assistant director has failed. It's time for Fred to move in and assert his authority. I do. I knock and explain firmly that all is ready and that each passing minute is costing a fortune. Errol, in costume and makeup, opens the door and, clearly tiddly, whispers that he needs a doctor. A doctor is sent for and I, to cover the delay, over-rehearse everyone. The doctor arrives and enters the star's dressing room. I shoot close-ups of Alexis and Sakall reacting to anything I can think of, extras at the bar showing fear and happiness, and many long shots of "general activity" in the saloon. Finally, I return to Flynn's dressing room and explain that the delay must cease. The door opens, a liquor-laden doctor stumbles out, and Flynn emerges—charming, as always, and now only slightly zonked—smiles, and confides in me that "doctors can't hold their liquor like they did in the old days."

The Hero

Does the name Audie Murphy ring a bell? It should. He was the most decorated American soldier of World War II. He earned thirty-five awards for his service in the infantry in Europe. In the 1945 battle of Holtzwihr in eastern France, the twenty-year-old second lieutenant ordered his outnumbered men to withdraw, then himself mounted a burning American tank destroyer and grabbed its machine gun. Wounded in the leg and exposed to enemy fire from three sides, he held off a Nazi unit of 250 men and six tanks for more than an hour. Every medal the army minted he got, including the Medal of Honor—so special that it is awarded, in many more cases than not, posthumously. A sharecropper before his army days, Audie, a short, extremely handsome, and always courteous young man, became a very capable and successful actor. Like Flynn, Murphy never accepted supervision—not by superior officers in the army or by studio executives. And as his star status increased, so did his disdain for "the front office" and "brass" of any sort.

In spite of his baby face, he had the most frightening eyes of anyone I've ever known. I was directing him in a modestly budgeted western (*Column South*) and focused a camera in extreme close-up fashion on his face as he, playing a Union officer, aimed his rifle at the Indian chief (played by Dennis Weaver) and warned him in these immortal words: "Mendigo, you and I have been friends. Don't force me to pull the trigger." I quickly called "Cut" and changed the camera angle. Just playacting, Audie would have scared everyone in the audience with that look of his.

Now that you remember Audie, let's see if you remember General Mark Clark. Does Anzio help? Okay, he was the boss army man when our soldiers invaded the "soft underbelly" of the Axis during World War II. Clark, a tall, attractive, personable representative of the Joint Chiefs of Staff, was a splendid example of the Pentagon's image at its best. But to Audie he was just another symbol of the brass. Audie showed how he felt about that—and only a Congressional Medal of Honor holder could do it.

Column South was on location on the back lot at Universal, and the script called for the Indians to attack the fort, which would be protected by an undermanned but courageous band of Union soldiers under the command of martinet Robert Sterling and his right-hand man, Audie Murphy. Long shots had been completed, stuntmen had fallen off their horses as directed, and lunch had been called before we were to move in for closer angles. Murphy and I regularly ate sandwiches and played horseshoes till it was time to resume work. During our lunch break, word came to me from the front office that General Mark Clark was on his way to the set, via studio limo—and, you may be sure, accompanied by a batch of studio photographers—to visit Audie Murphy.

I passed that word along to Audie and I'll never forget his reaction: "Fred, we'll continue to play horseshoes, the general will walk toward me with a big smile on his face and his hand extended, I'll look him directly in the eye, and his hand will drop to his side. Then he'll remember that every soldier in the army, including the Commander in Chief, is required

Bonzo is on the ~~left~~ right.

Bonzo learning his lines.

to salute first when he greets a Medal of Honor holder.'' The general arrived, smiled, extended his hand, waited a beat, Audie looked him in the eye, the general stood to attention, saluted, and only then was his salute returned.

Later I asked Murphy why. Very slowly he answered me: ''Too many soldiers, who didn't have to, died at Anzio.''

Sadly, Audie himself died at forty-six, still a hero but never a businessman. He quickly lost the fortune he made in Hollywood playing heroic characters.

The President

We are all aware that when someone is elected to ''the highest office in the land'' and is recognized as ''the leader of the Free World,'' that person has countless problems to face and enormous burdens to bear. No day dawns without the recognition that his every word and action, no matter how casual, will engender the closest scrutiny and evaluation. But no other president, from our first to our fortieth, has had to live with the knowledge, blameless as he may have been, that he starred—along with an extremely talented chimpanzee—in a motion picture entitled *Bedtime for Bonzo*.

In 1949 Universal assigned me to direct a picture about a college professor, an attractive baby-sitter, and a chimp. For those of you who managed to miss the picture, the screenplay, simply stated, described a professor who believes that a member of the ape family, properly brought up and treated exactly as if he were a child, could be trained to act and react precisely as if he were a human of the same age. Of course, the professor's colleagues would scoff, the baby-sitter would find the notion absurd and the

After *Bonzo* and before the presidency—Governor and Mrs. Ronald Reagan.

"child" abhorrent, and the chimp would be both a delight and a terrible problem. By fade-out, however, the professor would prove that his theory was a valid one, his colleagues would change their jeers to cheers, and the baby-sitter would be deeply in love with both the professor and the chimp/child. Walter Slezak played the lead scoffer, Diana Lynn was the lovely lady, Bonzo played himself, and the youthful believer that love could conquer all was—there's no use denying it—Ronald Reagan.

Although *Bedtime for Bonzo* was a box-office success, and led to *Bonzo Goes to College* and *Bonzo, Private Eye,* Ronnie shrewdly decided one Bonzo picture was enough. And until his entrance into the political arena, the movie had faded from everyone's mind and memory. But, when Reagan campaigned for the governorship of California and later for the presidency, the picture's title and his simian co-star afforded his opponents ammunition to poke fun at his stature as an actor and as a candidate for political office.

Naturally, I have been asked time and again if Reagan had given any indication that he had the White House in mind while we worked together. It would be nice to say that I was the first to know that he had his eyes, even then, on Pennsylvania Avenue. But it wouldn't be true. As the head of the Screen Actors' Guild, Ronnie (I'm more formal now) was an active and respected labor leader, articulate, and informed on all the issues of the day. It was during his marriage to Jane Wyman (they were my neighbors and we saw each other frequently), that I first noticed his considerable political savvy. I also noted that Jane found politics about as interesting as his second favorite topic—sports.

When we worked together he was a complete professional, a much more than competent performer, interested in his part and in the overall picture, an outstanding joke teller, and most cooperative. It was often said, "If you ask Ronnie what time it is, he'll tell you how to make a clock," but I found him to be good company, knowledgeable in many fields, blessed with a great sense of humor. He still has it . . . and I think I can prove it.

Mrs. de Cordova (I call her Janet when we're alone) and I have been on the Reagan "okay list" for a long time. Not the "in, in list," but kind of on the cusp. As a result, we've been invited to a few private and state gatherings in Washington. At one of these (honoring President Mubarak of Egypt), the formal proceedings ended with mutual toasts of friendship between the two heads of state. After dinner and before Itzhak Perlman entertained us all with his "magic violin," there was a half-hour of wandering through the public rooms. Janet and I strolled into the Red Room, where the President was chatting with a small group of dignitaries. He saw us, and beckoned us to join him. He then pointed to me and said, "Ladies and gentlemen, this is the man primarily responsible for my being the President of the United States." There were, you can be sure, a few startled glances. He continued: "That's the truth. If Fred hadn't directed me in that monkey picture, I'd still be in show business and someone else would be living here."

I guess you take your compliments where you find them.

The King

If I had to choose one single person who was as big a star in real life as he was on screen, no contest—it was Gable. No one ever said he was the best actor. Spencer Tracy in his time, Laurence Olivier in his, received the accolades. But on the screen and in Hollywood, there was just one King—Mr. Gable. You cast him in a picture, audiences went to see it. You invited him to a party, everyone showed up. One hostess wasn't having much luck putting an evening together, so she called Clark and told him she was giving a small dinner for Cary Grant, a close friend of Clark's. He accepted. She then phoned Cary and said she was inviting a select few in Gable's honor. Cary said that of course he'd be there. The lady then called everyone she wanted to impress and said that she was giving a party for her close friends Clark and Cary. It turned into a rather large dinner . . . quickly.

I went hunting with Gable, played golf with him, and had a drink or two with him. He was a first-class shot, a second-class golfer, and a third-class drinker. One evening I mentioned that evaluation to him. He smiled the Gable smile and said: "I can live with that; it's class four, five, and six I'm worried about."

Women adored him; men wanted to be like him. He may have had enemies—I just never met one. And wouldn't have wanted to.

Joanie Dearest

My number-one lady star wasn't the biggest favorite in town and, it turned out, wasn't too big a hit in her own family. I was her dialogue director on *Mildred Pierce*—for which she won an Academy Award—and her sometime escort and companion. And always her fan.

Miss Joan Crawford was really something! She looked like a movie star, dressed like one, lived like one . . . and had the ability to make her "boyfriends" feel like her co-stars.

I wasn't stupid enough to believe that I was her first

Miss Crawford and a devoted admirer.

choice among the available men in town, but it was
nice to be in the lineup even if you weren't the designated hitter. The pattern was consistent—a great deal
of attention and a number of invitations from her, followed by periods of silence and phone calls answered
"I'm sorry, Miss Crawford isn't available." Then a
gift with a note enclosed: "Forgive me, I've been so
stupid. Call me. Soon. Yours, Joan." It was great fun
. . . for a while.

Joan certainly knew how to make a man feel important. Before going out with you, she'd model several
outfits and ask you to choose the one you'd like her to
wear. She'd lay out her jewelry for your selection.

And whatever liquor was your favorite, it was hers, too. Some weeks it must have been pretty confusing for her.

At no time did I ever see her harsh with her children. She insisted that they be polite and well mannered, but never during my tenure were coat hangers used for anything but clothes. She instructed her son and daughter to address her escorts as Uncle. And the first indication to me that I might not be the only man in her life was when young Christopher met me at the door and welcomed me warmly as "Uncle Somebody." A long time later she introduced me to her last

Roz Russell: beautiful, bright, talented, and with a grown-up sense of humor.

husband as "Fred Somebody, an old friend of the family." A lot of new faces and new bodies have become glamour girls since Joan's heyday, but I doubt that anyone then was her equal, or will ever be, on or off screen, at what a movie star was meant to be.

Pretty and Witty

Probably the brightest and wittiest of the lady luminaries was Rosalind Russell. She read the newspapers thoroughly, not just the amusement pages. And she chose her scripts and friends carefully. After we worked together on *Roughly Speaking,* she sent me a photo inscribed: "To the second Freddie in my life." The first Freddie was her one and only husband, Broadway producer Freddie Brisson. He wasn't exactly everyone's favorite person, which may be why someone dubbed him the "Lizard of Roz."

The Queen

It's most likely that Greta Garbo, had she lived in a different neighborhood, would have been the most important woman in my life. I was once her dinner partner, found her to be as beautiful in person as on the screen, a humorous and charming conversationalist, and was as thrilled as you can imagine when she leaned close and asked me to escort her home after the party. It was a long wait till good-bye time, but it finally arrived. I did indeed take her home. She lived *directly* next door to the hostess. Our "romance" lasted two minutes and we never met again.

My First Lady

It's my calculated guess that everyone in the world, you included, would give a great deal to be able to erase something one did—an event, a phrase, a decision—but one can't. Okay, you didn't mean it to turn out the way it did. Okay, you weren't really responsible for the end result. Okay, it wasn't your fault. But it happened, and whenever it comes to mind, you are a little, or a lot, ashamed. You don't talk about it, and the chances are that no one else remembers anything about it; but every now and then you are reminded—and you wish you weren't. The chances are that, at the time, it affected someone else more than it did you, and that makes you more aware of your guilt. In my case, I brought grief to one of the most talented and gracious ladies in the world. And to make the pain a little more painful, she forgave me.

Let's set the stage. Royal families are a major part of history. A few of them still exist, mostly in ceremonial fashion. By divine right, their titles and trappings are passed on from one generation to the next, and birthright rather than talent is the determining factor. Exception: the Royal Family of the Theater—the Barrymores. From one generation to another, they handed on the traditional Barrymore apple to a daughter or a son, and the critics recognized them for what they were—the best.

At a special moment in time there were three, each an acknowledged master or mistress—John, Lionel, and Ethel. I knew them all, admired them, was accepted by each of them as a friend, and in the case of one, was responsible for considerable distress.

It all started during the cocktail hour at Miss Ethel Barrymore's ranch-style home overlooking the Riviera Country Club in Pacific Palisades, California. I had finished a round of golf with Sammy Colt (Miss Barrymore's son by, as they say, Russell Colt of the firearms family) and he asked me to join him for a drink at his mother's nearby home. I did . . . and I wish I hadn't.

The "Happy Hour" was a pleasant one, made more so when the First Lady of the Stage joined us. She was charming, worldly, occasionally caustic in the Barrymore tradition, and considerably more frail than the last time I'd seen her. I enjoyed her charm, her worldliness, was entertained by her sarcastic comments, and chose, selfishly, to ignore the frailty. Because I had an ax to grind.

Universal had purchased a screenplay that featured in the starring roles a child of three and a clever and conniving grandmother. Finding the proper performers posed a considerable problem, which no one at the studio had been able to solve. I figured that if I could sweet-talk Miss Barrymore into reading the script, convince her that it would be a wonderful comeback role, get her to agree to play it, I would be assigned the plum directorial assignment.

She ultimately read the script and liked it, but felt that the part was far too physically demanding. She thanked me for thinking of her but, if she was to be realistic, had to say no.

I put a lot of pressure on her, explaining that she could trust me to solve all the problems, and she agreed. Because she had confidence in me.

The studio was delighted, gave us a start date, and released a barrage of publicity: a Barrymore was "returning to the screen." We found the required youngster (there's an abundance of intelligent three-year-old actors; it's later they grow up to be stupid), and *Finders Keepers* went into production.

Three days of shooting made it crystal clear it

wouldn't work. Miss Barrymore's magnificent voice and her commanding presence were there—but, more important, her timing wasn't. Her movements were hesitant, shaky. Very quickly two people recognized that a mistake had been made—Miss Barrymore and I. After the third filming day, the lady asked me to visit with her in her dressing room to discuss the situation. And please read carefully what she proposed: *she* would go to the studio executives and explain that she had *asked* to play the part but now realized she wasn't up to it and would like to release them from any and all commitments. That way she felt that no blame would fall on my shoulders. She said that her reputation was secure, but mine would be damaged. It worked out just as she planned.

Hedda Hopper and Louella Parsons tried their best to get her to say she had been "used and humiliated" by me, but she stuck to her story.

On or off the screen, for me, there will be only *one* First Lady—Ethel Barrymore.

Judy—Judy—Judy!

You're a star on the stage, in pictures, on TV. You make a fortune every week. Trade papers, magazines, and Barbara Walters all report your popularity. You live in a mansion, your wife loves you, and your children are clean, decent, and don't do drugs. You have every reason to be happy and secure. But it's one to ten that you're insecure.

And it's easy to understand why. If you tell jokes for a living, you worry that the audiences won't laugh. If you're a beauty, you know that aging brings wrinkles. If you're a sports legend, you are aware that the legs go first. If you're a singer, the high notes grow

A very young Judy Garland and a rather young F de C, very happy to be with her.

higher. If you act, so does that new up-and-coming young guy or gal.

I've had dozens of opportunities to see, close up, how the coolest of stars turn into Jell-O before the curtain goes up. Even the most self-possessed are delighted when the first laugh is heard or when a hush greets a tense scene. When you earn a living as a performer, the performance itself is, if all goes well, the safety zone. "Before" is worry time; "after," you tread water till the next time.

One comedian was so nervous he would regularly twist his jacket buttons till they broke off. A major

A young Fred and a young Judy.

stage star would excuse himself before his first entrance, saying, "I'll be back in a minute; it's time for me to throw up."

Of everyone I've known, however, one outstandingly talented young lady was the most insecure of all. I truly believe that everyone in the world loved Judy Garland—but Judy Garland.

We first met in New York when she was sent there on a publicity tour. The Brass at MGM chose where she was to go and by whom she would be escorted. I was one of those chosen, and our first evening together was a rather memorable one—the premiere of *Pal Joey,* the night that Gene Kelly became an overnight sensation. After the show we went backstage and asked Gene to join us at the Copacabana, he gladly accepted, and a long-lasting three-way friendship began.

Later, in Hollywood, Judy was the first star I visited on a set. She was warm and charming. We went dining and dancing on a number of occasions. I sincerely hoped her warmth and charm might escalate to a higher plateau, but she firmly and graciously informed me that we'd gone about as far as we were going to go. Judy's mother, however, informed me that one of Judy's sisters was less restrictive in her thinking. Judy was present when that comment was made—which may give you an insight into the happy home life of a star.

I don't think I ever saw Judy Garland in her happy days or her depressed ones that I wasn't stunned by her talent and, at the same time, aware of the sadness behind her smile.

As the years passed, I spent time with her when she was Mrs. Vincente Minnelli and later Mrs. Sid Luft. She often asked if her sister had been more than warm and charming. Judy was completely aware of her inability to "cope" and delighted in telling stories highlighting her "goofs." My favorite involved a meeting she insisted on having with the Master of Metro, Mr. Louis B. Mayer, when she felt she had a number of grievances about the studio's treatment of her and wanted to explain the problems to him personally—without her agents—and hoped that, in spite of her awe and fear of Mayer, her sincerity would make him understand.

They met in his extremely imposing office. She was nervous. He was brusque. She became more nervous. Mayer removed his glasses and stared at her. Judy decided to break the tension:

JUDY: My, it's hot today.
(Mayer nods)
JUDY: But it was even hotter yesterday.
(Mayer nods again)
JUDY: I guess the day before was the hottest of all.
(Mayer stands up, puts his glasses back on)
MAYER: Judy, just what was it you wanted to tell me?
(Judy stands bravely, decides it's now or never)
JUDY: I think the time has come to tell you . . .
(Mayer stares and Judy panics)
JUDY: That . . . that . . . I've been in heat all week.

Judy heard her words and ran out of the office.

Judy panicked too often, compensated for her fears with drugs and liquor—and left us all much too soon.

Macho Man

In the early days of his career, I directed Rock Hudson in a few of his less memorable movies. Raoul Walsh, a splendid director of action pictures, had made a screen test of an aspiring actor named Roy Fitzgerald and suggested that Universal sign the tall, dark, and handsome young man to a contract. They did. We met while I was on location shooting an Yvonne DeCarlo classic in Tucson. Rock was fascinated by the movie world, and it was obvious that he had all the requisites for a sizable career. At Universal I directed him in a light comedy, *Peggy,* and I teamed him with Jackie Gleason as "henchmen of the Caliph" in the costume epic *The Desert Hawk.* We enjoyed working together. After filming one day, I told him of an absurd and unattractive remark I'd heard from one of his friends: "You know, of course, that Rock is gay." I turned on the rumor monger and told him he should be ashamed of himself for spreading such a ridiculous story. The man insisted his information was accurate, and I told Rock I had bet the guy five hundred dollars he was wrong.

Rock thanked me for defending his reputation, but told me he'd like to have half of the other guy's bet. You win a few and you lose a few.

PART THREE

Mostly Me

Parental Guidance
Suggested

No autobiography can be deemed complete without the obligatory chapter devoted to the parents of the author and how much his career was influenced by the love and attention lavished on him by his mother and father during his formative years. Or how he finally overcame the scars of rejection received while he was a child.

In most cases, we learn that he came from poor but honest parents. Therefore, there was no way to go but up. Okay, Henry Ford II was an exception. I would be pleased in this parental chapter to join the others and claim that my mother and father were poor but honest, but that would be a considerable deviation from the truth.

Actually, I was born in rather lavish surroundings. An apartment on the corner of Sixty-fourth Street and Park Avenue was even then a most fashionable address in New York City. On that fateful day in 1910, the de Cordovas were living high on the hog . . . and they managed to function in that manner for most of my early years. With a few distressing interludes.

The time has come to admit that my father, George de Cordova—also known as Albert Martini, Charles Salmi, Max Rothschild (to name a few variations on the theme)—earned his living "by his wits." He was, as they say, a confidence man, and from what I was told and what I saw, he was a remarkably able and successful one. *The Guinness Book of World Records* doesn't contain a list of the Ten Best Swindlers; but scam experts say that if it did, my dad would be right at the top.

Nicky Arnstein was once married to stage star Fanny Brice. You probably recall that Omar Sharif and Barbra Streisand portrayed them in the motion picture *Funny Girl*. Mr. Arnstein was often referred to on newspaper front pages as an "alleged master swindler." He told me that my father was in a class by himself. Praise from Caesar!

Dad, I eventually learned, played more parts than a repertory actor. Sometimes he was "with the government"; often he was the roving editor of the official travel guide, Baedeker; frequently he was the exploratory executive of a mining conglomerate; and now and then he was a retired financier with many investment irons still in the fire. All his "occupations" allowed him to appear a bit secretive, and all required that he be able to depart his surroundings quickly, without lengthy explanations. Somehow he had the ability to *be* the man he was pretending to be and could discuss, knowledgeably, the inner secrets and corporate workings of whatever business he was pretending to be in charge of at that moment.

My mother, Margaret Veronica Timmins (Martini, Salmi, Rothschild, *et al.*) was equally versatile. She was the perfect leading lady in all my father's escapades and shifted gears—and backgrounds—with no apparent problem. She was an extremely attractive woman (a show girl in many Shubert and a few Ziegfeld musicals) and remained so even as the years went by. She combined an earthy Irish sense of humor with an air of innocence and naïveté, which made her the perfect companion for her husband's many personas and roles.

When George married Margy, I am told, he explained that his precarious method of making a living would cause their life-style to be "chicken one day and feathers the next." She knew what he meant—if not the details, at least the overall picture was clear—and for fifty years they had a high old time together. They really loved each other, shared the good and bad times together, and made sure—together—that I would never do anything even slightly dishonest. You see, both of them knew that no matter how happy and at ease my father seemed, he hated what he did. I told you they weren't honest, but I'm sure you would have loved them. Everybody did. Most of all me.

Our family lived "high line" most of the time. Home base was in most cases a hotel. We usually "followed the sun," and I spent most of my formative years in the most luxurious summer and winter resorts extant: in Florida at the Coral Gables Biltmore or The Breakers; in California at the Del Monte Lodge or the Del Coronado near San Diego; in Michigan at Mackinac's Grand Hotel; in Minnesota at Breezy Point Lodge—to name an expensive few. In New York City, it was at the Ritz Carlton; in Chicago, the Drake; in Los Angeles, at the Ambassador; in Philadelphia, at the Warwick; and in Europe, at all the proper and fashionable establishments. Only twice did Mother and I stay in cheap and unattractive hotels—when circumstances dictated that we be as close as possible to a jail.

The family modus operandi was generally the same. Usually, and always with the finest of luggage and with the remaining proceeds from the last scam, we would check into our new digs and request the most desirable accommodations. We would shortly thereafter become close friends with a number of our fellow guests (who were invariably charmed by my parents), entertain with no apparent regard for the cost, use all the facilities—hire the motor launches, engage the fishing guides, arrange golf instruction for Fred—accept invitations (or extend them) to friendly card games, order the finest wines, lay out just-this-side-of-lavish tips, and occasionally at first, then more frequently—sign for everything.

Ordinarily, there was enough cash to pay for everything . . . for a period of time. If Mr. Whatever returned from one of his frequent trips "to the plant" with a new bundle of dividends, there was, of course, no problem at all. But if that was not the case, nothing would appear to be different. However, we knew that checkout time was not too far away. Before long an emergency phone call would arrive, very unhappily we would have to cut our happy vacation short, Dad would hurriedly instruct the hotel cashier to forward the balance of our bill to the head office of his business firm or to the hotel we would shortly be checking into. That would, of course, be another well-known, first-class establishment, and the good-bye tips that were spread around were always just large enough to make it seem absurd that "forward the balance of my bill" was anything but Dad's way of doing things. Keep in mind that American Express and Diners Club cards hadn't been invented yet.

I've always been fascinated by the next step in the process. After we had been in residence in our new location and after Dad had made a new strike in a new operation, an indignant letter of protest would be sent to our previous hotel complaining that their negligence in forwarding our bill was causing a problem for our auditors. By the time the bill arrived—for the *third* time—there was no problem paying off the old tab. While we were running up some new accounts.

Once in a while, nothing went well. Old accounts remained unpaid, the new indebtedness was growing, and the current enterprise hadn't begun to pay dividends. We were, it appeared, close to the edge. Phase three was put into operation. Both Mother and Dad began to find the service at our hotel unacceptable: the waiters were clumsy; phone messages were not being delivered promptly; doors were left unlocked and clothes were missing from our closets. We were just fed up with the way the hotel was being run. Politely but firmly the manager was informed that too many mistakes had been made, Mother (trying to calm Father) and I were told to pack our belongings immediately, reservations were made at another hotel about five blocks away, the cashier was instructed to transfer our account without delay, and we stomped out in seeming anger—only to break out in laughter during the taxi ride to our new address. Fortunately, before long a gullible investor would display financial interest in Dad's newest venture, our funds would be replenished, old bills would be paid, and again we would be solvent . . . for the moment.

Soon we would receive a letter of apology from the manager of the hotel that had treated us "so shabbily," expressing the hope that in the near future we would return and notice the improvement in the service. Of course, when the time was expedient, we *would* return. Why hold a grudge?

Just exactly what did this father of mine do, you ask, to feather our nest so luxuriously and stay "at liberty" while fleecing his sheep? How did he keep the balls in the air for so long? Why didn't the other shoe drop? Well, you should keep in mind that all his actions took place a long time ago and what he did has often been done by others in the ensuing years. But what he did, he did first and he did it well.

For instance, he would option some wilderness land and "salt it" with nuggets of gold and arrange for an assay report that would in fact confirm the existence of a good deal of precious metal in the area. He'd print stock certificates and sell shares in the "Goldfield Daisy" lode, the stock would be sold, and a digging date would be set in the not-too-distant future. Shortly before that deadline he'd provide himself with an escape hatch—once he took a hunting knife, severely gashed his leg and stumbled to the nearest newspaper office with the story that poachers had attacked him and damn near killed him in an attempt to take over the claim. He wasn't frightened, he would explain; but to hell with the gold, he'd sell his stock for ten cents on the dollar. No amount of money was important enough to cut short his life and the happiness he enjoyed with his wife and child. The suckers grabbed the bait, bought him out, he hightailed it out of the region and was, I assume, as unhappy as they when it turned out that the land wasn't as valuable as the first reports had indicated. From a safe—and considerable—distance, of course.

It's probably true, chronologically speaking, that a man named Ponzi invented the "pyramid scheme"; at least he has received the credit for it. But if he was the first, Dad was the second. And a simple setup it was, and still is. An investment expert appears in the area where you live and guarantees extremely high returns to those who supply him funds in exchange for his expertise and "insider knowledge" of the working of the stock market or the real estate field or of farm conditions. The early participants did indeed reap high returns on their investment—paid to them, of course, from the investments of those who came along later.

Mother and Dad at the Stork Club—probably between scams.

Oddly enough, Dad's business acumen often kept the pyramid going for amazing lengths of time, which is probably why Charles Ponzi, who didn't have that expertise, received the credit for the sting and did the jail time, while my father, again, stayed free and clear. Mrs. de Cordova played a minor but important histrionic role during this operation by regularly bursting into the maestro's well-filled office on strategically planned occasions, tears of joy streaming down her cheeks, loudly exclaiming that his advice had made her a rich and happy woman. Even before E. F. Hutton, people listened.

Then there was the over-investor scheme, which was successful in many areas but worked best of all in the New York theater world. It goes something like this: A shrewd producer options a script from a promising author; word is spread in the proper places that any number of important stars would "kill" to play the leading roles, and that many show-wise investors are anxious to "come aboard." Because of all this interest and pressure, the primary owner/discoverer (guess who) reluctantly agrees to sell a small portion of his interest . . . and another small portion, etc., etc., etc. Somehow or other he *reluctantly,* mind you, manages to dispose of three or four hundred percent of the ownership. And just has to sit back and enjoy (while shedding industrial-strength tears of disappointment) the reviews of New York's cruel and biased critics who make mincemeat of the production. It was always possible, of course, that the newspapers might find the play to be amusing and entertaining; but if you check the success-to-failure odds, you'll quickly realize that Las Vegas offers a much better deal. Add a little stacking to the deck—improper casting (those major stars just weren't available)—and the value of underrehearsing, plus scheduling the opening night during the summer months. When the play was a failure and closed abruptly, no one was more depressed at the blatant stupidity of the critics than Mr. Four Hundred Percent.

Success in this scheme depended, as you realize, on my father's ability to select a script that had enough merit to attract interest but not enough overall quality to warrant success at the box office. He had that ability. But, oddly enough, he wasn't so perceptive years later when I was able to arrange for him to buy into *Hellzapoppin'* and *Oklahoma.* He had no faith in either. But thank God he didn't try the four-hundred-percent plan on either of those productions. We'd still be paying off or hiding in the Andes.

I mentioned some pages ago that on two occasions jail came into our lives. And so it did, but even Babe Ruth didn't hit a home run every time he went to bat. I have no desire to belittle any of the trusting folks who believed in, and were taken in by, my father's schemes, but only twice, and far from the scene of the crime, did his victims recognize him and report their discovery to the authorities. Both times he was taken into custody. Naturally he denied that he was the person involved, but in both instances he was bound over while the accusations were being investigated. In those days, it took a longer time to check things out than it does now, and that delay was vital to the accused.

Father always carried, "just in case," the *exact* number of bichloride of mercury tablets—one more would have killed him—and both times he was in custody, he swallowed the tablets. He was taken from his cell and rushed to the hospital ward, where, lo and behold, an attractive nurse skilled in the treatment of ingested poison came upon the scene. Immediately she ascertained that the patient's condition required more elaborate attention than the jail hospital could provide, displayed her credentials, called an ambulance and arranged for him to be taken to a more complete hospital, and rode with him in the ambulance—to our nearby hotel, where she administered the always-ready antidote. Shortly afterward, the suspect and Florence Nightingale departed the area quickly and forever. They were accompanied by a rather bewildered and worried son.

I continue to stress that neither of my parents was proud of these activities, nor should they have been. People were, and there's no other word for it, swindled by what they did. But if the "perfect scheme" had worked, it is likely that everything would have been different. And it damn near worked. It was, according to those who knew about it, flawless. Try this on for size—and dissolve to long ago.

A young New Yorker who had visited, and was enchanted by, California decided to open the West to easterners and became rich in so doing. He invested his meager bankroll in a series of ads in *The New York Times*. They read:

Subscribe to California's favorite magazine. Learn all about the Land of the Future. Send five dollars and receive twelve editions of *Your Western Friend* plus outright ownership of one acre of California land with perpetual water rights. Don't delay. Send your check today.

He paid for the ad and set out for San Francisco— after all, he had to start printing an as yet nonexistent magazine.

California, you must keep in mind, was a never-never land in those days. New York curiosity was high, and a magazine subscription plus an ownership of land for a mere five dollars sounded like a good deal. An amazing amount of mail began arriving at the headquarters of *Your Western Friend*—my father's hotel room. He left the envelopes unopened, placed them in two large valises, and carried them to the office of one of San Francisco's bankers—the appointment gained by explaining that a large deposit was about to be made. The banker was genuinely impressed when the contents of the luggage were dumped on his desk and he was asked to open any, or all, of the envelopes. He found that each one contained a check or a five-dollar bill plus a letter indicating an interest in California and a desire to share in its future. Very quickly the banker agreed to the following procedure:

1. The bank would arrange for the use of printing presses for the about-to-begin-to-be-published magazine. The contents would at first be pasteup articles gleaned from any source, as long as it praised the state

of California. Also, there would be numerous replicas of the advertisement originally run in *The New York Times*.

2. With one dollar of each five received, the banker would advance a dollar for the purchase of acreage in the San Joaquin Valley—a dollar an acre being the going price for wasteland miles away from the nearest drop of water. And for his time and interest in the future of his beloved state, the banker would put another dollar in his own pocket.

3. From each five dollars there was, thus, this breakdown:

> 1 dollar to the banker
> 1 dollar for the land purchase
> 1 dollar to publish the magazine
> 2 dollars to the man behind the plan:
>> 1 dollar for living expenses
>> and
>> 1 dollar to purchase land in
>> his own name.

Why was it the perfect scheme? Observe. The magazine progressed from its original reprint material and became, by virtue of articles written by respected California-oriented authors, a successful and accepted publication. As the circulation grew, the stream of responses to the advertisements grew as well—and the money arrived in continually increasing amounts.

And, as a result, more and more land was purchased and trust deeds and maps were mailed to all investors. Each did, in fact, own an acre of California land.

When enough money had been accumulated, the major move took place. If the wasteland was to become truly valuable it had to be transformed into verdant farmland. That could come about only if water was available. A dam was the logical solution.

And so, as the Bible says, it came to pass. Funds were funneled into the proper channels—and to the proper people—and construction of the dam began. News of this development spread quickly, and everyone became aware that when the dam was completed, the arid land would be fertile, and all those who had purchased perpetual water rights would be owners of land whose value would increase a hundredfold. Requests to "get in" became overwhelming, the price per acre tripled, and the most envied man on the Coast was the largest single owner of land in the San Joaquin Valley. Guess who it was.

At the height of his success, my father, accompanied by opera star Enrico Caruso and several of the city's most beautiful ladies, entered the Diamond Bar on Market Street in San Francisco. En route to their table, Dad dropped a silver dollar into a slot machine, saying to the bartender, "If I hit the jackpot, it's yours." Three bars crossed the face of the machine, silver dollars spouted from the payoff mouth, and the bartender shouted, "Mr. de, your luck is beyond belief! Nothing can stop you but an earthquake!" That was, as you've surmised, the night of April 17, 1906. In the next few hours the word "earthquake" became a part of the American language. San Francisco was destroyed; the partially built dam crumbled, and with it, the Perfect Scheme. There was no dam, no water, and the last thing easterners cared about was land in California—or its future. The bartender was one hundred percent correct: "nothing but an earthquake."

Before we wrap the story on George and Margaret de Cordova, I should point out the happy ending. As soon as my show-business salary allowed me to make the decision, I took them to dinner at "21," toasted them with champagne, and retired them. There were to be no more escapades—from that night on, honesty was now the best and only policy. I would take over as head of the household, and the future would be less exciting, perhaps, but considerably more carefree. No three people were ever as delighted. Mother and Dad moved to California with me, lived to acceptably ripe old ages, and became respected and contributing members of the community, and both would have been highly pleased at the celebrity turnouts for their funerals.

They've been gone for quite a while now, but I still tear up a bit when so many people say they remember my parents and: "Weren't they a wonderful couple!"

Onward and
(Sometimes) Upward

My adult life, somewhat like Gaul, can be divided
into four parts:

1. The Broadway Days
2. The Movie Years
3. The Television Times
4. What Is Still to Come

It is logical to assume that Part 4 may not last as long
as the others, but I'll make every effort to see that it
does.

In retrospect, it's surprising how smoothly one era
blended into the next, and at the risk of sounding like
a male Pollyanna, I'm aware that I've had more good
times and more good friends than anyone is entitled
to. Through the years it is clear—clearer since I
started to write this book—that I've lived a charmed
life. Although I've moved so often from one project to
another and from one circle of close associates to another, I believe that a major factor in my overall happiness is that what came next in each case was even
more rewarding than what came before. Each move,

whether or not my choice, turned out to be the right one, and no step upward seemed such a big one that I felt the pressure to be a problem.

I'm truly grateful that I didn't have a blazing beginning—no smashing early success. So many talented artists shone so brightly, so quickly, and never were able to match what they did when first they burst into prominence and were acclaimed by one and all. Think back on Orson Welles, and James Dean, Marilyn Monroe, and Montgomery Clift, for example. They climbed so high, so early, and found that the Top was where they were and from Up, there was no way to go but Down.

Of course, there are exceptions—talents who made it early in their lives and for a long time managed to move from one success to another; but most of them made a monumental mistake—they kept on living and the parade passed them by. Just read the credits of Mervyn LeRoy: *Little Caesar, I Am a Fugitive from a Chain Gang, Wizard of Oz, Tugboat Annie, Quo Vadis?, Mr. Roberts!* Hard to do better than that; but eventually the scripts stopped coming because some executives decided that a new boy might have a different, more current slant on what the public wanted.

Probably the brightest, wittiest, most inventive director of them all is Billy Wilder. He's responsible for such triumphs as: *Double Indemnity, Some Like It Hot, The Apartment, Sunset Boulevard, Lost Weekend,* and *Irma La Douce.* But *Kiss Me, Stupid* and *Avanti* and *Buddy, Buddy* weren't exactly blockbusters, and some of the Brass decided they'd check the availability of ''that kid who does those great commercials'' before they'd talk to Wilder. In his case there's a difference: he never wanted to talk to them.

Vincente Minnelli directed *Meet Me in St. Louis, An American in Paris, Father of the Bride, Gigi, The Band Wagon, The Bad and the Beautiful,* and *Lust for*

Life. It's hard to believe, but long before he died, the phone stopped ringing.

Granted that these legends are rightly respected and appreciated by their peers and regularly have received medals and awards at one film festival after another, I feel some consolation in knowing that if you never flew so high, you never had so far to fall.

We've been talking giants, but sadder by far are the instant television stars of both sexes who, when the first episode of a new series is at the top of the Nielsen ratings, are embraced as the greatest possible additions to the world of entertainment. It doesn't take long for the public to turn the channel selector, and the additions are quickly subtracted. Of course, many performers overcome the stigma of a failed series and reappear the next season; but the fuzz is mostly off the peach.

Certainly there have been survivors, and deservedly so. Helen Hayes, Claudette Colbert, Barbara Stanwyck, Katharine Hepburn, Laurence Olivier, John Gielgud—they have all been on top, tottered a bit on occasion, but regained their balance, adjusted to the passing of time, and remain respected and revered. Jack Lemmon, Gregory Peck, Bob Hope, Walter Matthau, Jimmy Stewart, and, yes, Johnny Carson *were* stars and *are* stars. They made it early and they made it often. But they are the few. So many others became overnight sensations, flared, sputtered, and were gone.

No one said that fame is forever, but I'm distressed when I read that George Gobel is playing a luncheon gig outside San Diego or that Donald O'Connor is appearing as Captain Andy in a dinner-theater production of *Showboat*. There's nothing wrong with earning an honest living after the spotlight has dimmed, but there's a lot of heartache involved when a real estate agent hawks a home as "the *former* estate of . . . "

Now that we've established that my long and mediocre career has brought me satisfaction and contentment, I hasten to explain that the places I've been and the people I've known are the reason.

Let's start with Broadway, which, like Hollywood or the Windy City, shouldn't be thought of in geographical terms; it's a state of mind. The Big Apple, Mazda Lane, Gotham City, Bagdad on the Hudson, or just New York, New York—love it or leave it, believe me there's never been another place like it. It isn't, and wasn't, just the theaters and restaurants, Fifth Avenue, the Yankees and, once upon a time, the Giants and Dodgers; it's the people. Most of them aren't born there, but it doesn't take long before they're New Yorkers—and everybody else isn't. Sure, being from the South or the West, including Texas, is a source of pride to those who hail from those worthy areas; but we all know about Forty-second Street, we know "the Bronx is Up and the Battery's Down," and it's really true that "Every Street's a Boulevard in Old New York."

I arrived on the scene during the salad days. You are aware, if you've paid strict attention, that I was no stranger to New York. But starting in 1932 it became my, not my parents', town. I became a part of it and as quickly as I could—and some strange and remarkable people "took me in" and my love affair with the city began immediately.

Okay, I'm a graduate (medium laude) of Northwestern University, I've finished Harvard Law School, and Johnny Shubert has given me a job as his assistant in the Shubert Theatrical Enterprises. Obviously I'm well on my way. Well, not exactly. An organizational chart of the Shubert empire may help to clarify my status. Lee Shubert and J. J. Shubert were brothers— like Cain and Abel were brothers. They barely spoke to each other, disapproved of every production decision made by the other, and maintained separate offices in separate buildings.

J.J. was headquartered on the fifth floor of the Sardi Building on West Forty-fourth Street and lived in a luxurious and tastefully furnished penthouse on top of the building—which he owned. Lee operated from the top floor of the Shubert Theater, across the street from the Sardi Building, and lived in a super penthouse atop an apartment building—which he owned—on Central Park West. Their chauffeurs and their limousines parked side by side in Shubert Alley, a private cross street between Forty-fourth and Forty-fifth streets—which, of course, they owned.

Lee Shubert was childless. J.J.'s only child was my very close friend and law school chum, John. You might expect that he would, as the only heir, be embraced by both his father and his uncle. To whom else would they pass the baton? Actually, each looked upon him as an interloper and a rival and delegated no responsibilities to him, second-guessed him on his every suggestion, and made it clear to all employees that their one and only successor was to have no place in the corporate decisions. You can imagine the importance attached to the thoughts and suggestions of his best friend and associate, Fred.

J.J.'s vast personal office wasn't easy to reach. His two secretaries shared a strategically placed area directly adjacent to it, and the offices of his casting director and script evaluator were next in line. Johnny was assigned an office of his own, but had to traverse three sets of associates in order to make personal contact with his father. I was assigned a desk near the rest room—but not the executive rest room.

I was, however, quickly pressed into service. Mr. J.J. chose me as his personal messenger. Regularly I would be called into his office and instructed to go across the street and tell "that idiot brother of mine that he's just made the stupidest decision of his life and that I'll see him in court before I sign the deal. Tell him he's a fool and everyone knows it. Then hurry crosstown and cancel the order my stupid son made for all that fabric. Then get right back here." With a "Yes, sir, Mr. J.J.," I ran to the elevator, crossed the street, went up to Mr. Lee's office, and found myself face to face with the "idiot brother." I delivered Mr. J.J.'s message verbatim—sort of: "Mr. Lee, Mr. J.J. would like to take a little more time to think over your suggestion and hopes you'll discuss it further." Solved, right?

Mr. Lee's answer: "Son, explain to my idiot brother that I was *informing* him of my decision, not asking for his approval, and that if he wants to discuss anything with me, he can ask for an appointment."

"Got it, Mr. Lee," I said, and hurried on my crosstown errand, as instructed, only to realize I had no idea where I was supposed to go and what fabric I was supposed to cancel.

Some generous-minded people have been nice enough to say that my "translations" of the "tell-my-idiot-brother" messages played a definite part in bringing Mr. Lee and Mr. J.J. closer together. I rather doubt it. I remember that immediately after I'd directed my first picture for Warner's I was sent by the studio on a promotional junket. During my stay in New York I decided to visit the Shubert offices, was ushered into J.J.'s office, congratulated by him on the reviews of my picture, and told to hurry across the street and tell his idiot brother that I was one more proof he'd never known talent and never would.

Back to my friend and sponsor, Johnny Shubert. Don't feel too sorry for him: he was very attractive, extremely wealthy, and well aware that eventually he would "get it all." He was charming enough and bright enough to become, as time passed, a vital figure in the Shubert hierarchy and the entire theatrical world—and he had three very close friends: Eddie Dowling, Abe Cohen, and me. Not too imposing a list, I agree. But we were very close and we had fun.

Dowling went to Columbia University on an athletic scholarship, wasn't very interested in class work, flunked out, and became a "gypsy" in the chorus line of several Shubert musicals. He moved up to stage managing and eventually became the general stage manager for all the Shubert shows. There were about ten of them a year. He would be the backstage boss during the rehearsal period, go on the road during the tryout and revision weeks, stay with the production for the New York opening, then turn over the job to an assistant and move on to the next extravaganza. Like an army sergeant, he was top dog of the backstage troops and the boss of everyone his side of the curtain. About eighty percent of the "troops" were the loveliest-looking dancers and show girls in town. A tough job—but someone had to do it.

As a collegian, Johnny Shubert quickly learned that Dowling was the perfect entree into the world of backstage beauty. They became friends, then close pals; worldly-wise Eddie was Johnny's advisor and mentor in opening the fun side of the business to the boss's son. Dowling was street smart, charming, alternately bellicose and friendly, and very happy with his status as Johnny's closest friend. He drank a lot—on some occasions without starting a fight.

Abe Cohen was Dowling's counterpart on the other side of the curtain. A company manager is the financial representative of a production company, in charge of ticket sales, transportation, payrolls, advertising, hotel accommodations—every place where money is spent or saved. Abe, like Eddie, was the number-one Shubert man in his area. He too moved from one production to another, and inasmuch as most Shubert shows opened in Philadelphia and Boston, and inasmuch as Johnny attended the University of Pennsylvania (in Philadelphia) and Harvard (in Boston), and inasmuch as Eddie and Abe were longtime close friends, Abe also became an advisor and associate of the theatrical scion.

Johnny, Eddie, and Abe enjoyed their palship, and with young Shubert about to move from school to active participation in the firm, neither Eddie nor Abe needed the addition of a new best friend. But there I was—and they were less than ecstatic.

Feeling, as I certainly did, that there wasn't a great future in crossing the street to mediate in internecine warfare, I asked Johnny to move me from my office job into the production field. He managed to get my request okayed and I was assigned to stage-manage the next Winter Garden musical, *Hold Your Horses,* starring Joe Cook, Dave Chasen, and Ona Munson (remember Belle Watling in *Gone With the Wind*?). Dowling was my supervisor; Abe was the company manager. I was rather insecure about what I was supposed to do; after all, I was functioning in enemy territory. Add that it was a J. J. Shubert production— and *he* didn't have too much regard for me, either.

I walked as straight a line as possible, saved Dowling from being sucker-punched by coldcocking a drunken stagehand, did Abe's payroll duties one early morning after he'd been overserved the night before, and actually put my life and my job in jeopardy by challenging J.J. in front of the entire cast when he made a snide remark about his son. Attitudes shifted, and a few days before the show was to entrain for the Boston opening, Dowling suggested that the four of us have some drinks at Billy La Hiff's Tavern. I felt that I, like d'Artagnan, had been accepted into the Musketeers.

La Hiff's—which later became Toots Shor's Tavern

—was a popular dining and drinking gathering place. It did a ton of business, but unless you were a "regular," you sat in the back. Up front you were liable to see New York's "Night Mayor" Jimmy Walker, Georgie Jessel, Walter Winchell, Mark Hellinger, Damon Runyon, Ethel Merman, Ted Husing, Joe DiMaggio, Bert Lahr, Tallulah Bankhead, and a smattering of gracious and well-groomed hoodlums. As quickly as possible I made La Hiff's my hangout, and I'll never forget when James J. Walker noticed me at the bar, beckoned me over to his table, and said, "Son, if you're alone, why don't you sit down here." I know that Governor Roosevelt caught the Mayor with his fingers in the cookie jar, but I'll never forget the man who wrote "Will You Love Me in September As You Did in May" and who got me accepted in the "up-front" area at Billy La Hiff's.

Some of the best times of my life involved the Tavern and the people I met there. There was Jessel, "The Toastmaster General of the United States"— probably the greatest raconteur I've ever known and a big vaudeville star. Down the line I directed him and Sophie Tucker in *High Kickers*—not the biggest hit in Broadway history. George and I played gin every chance we got, we kept a running score, and when the show closed, I wrote a check to him for a hefty amount. He took it, folded it neatly, folded it again, and tore it up, saying, "You're too good a director and too bad a gin player for me to accept this." Years later in Hollywood I beat George at gin for an even larger sum and had the fun of tearing up his check. I waited a long time to be able to say, "My directing never got any better, but my gin game did."

Damon Runyon was a legend as a sports writer. He knew all there was to know about athletic events, the athletes themselves, and the strange people who hang around them. His *Guys and Dolls* is a good example.

I directed George Jessel in *High Kickers* on Broadway in 1941. He was the best storyteller I've ever known. But he turned down *The Jazz Singer* picture and a fellow called Al Jolson agreed to do it.

Runyon had, indeed, a way with words. Case in point: Just before I "left" Warner's I was phoned by a Universal producer, Leonard Goldstein, who had a script he thought I might like to read. I called Mr. Runyon (then a top screenwriter in Hollywood) and asked him for a rundown on this Mr. Goldstein. Damon explained things this way: "Fred, you know that Universal is run by two men, Billy Goetz and Leo Spitz." I did know that. "Well," Damon continued, "Goldstein is very important to them—he gets for Spitz and spits for Goetz."

And Mark Hellinger. Where to start! He wrote a daily column for the *New York Mirror,* in the O. Henry style—the end of every story had a surprise twist. He was an impeccable dresser (his shirts and ties were made of the same material and color); he spoke as you'd expect a newspaperman to speak and was never flustered or irritated—unless you tried to pick up a check in his presence. Lots of people tried to; nobody could.

His word was his bond and he was totally trusted by everyone. Case in point: One night at La Hiff's he was called to the phone, returned to the table, and explained he had to leave to cover a story. Years later we learned the details. The phone call had been from "Mad Dog" Coll (a very dangerous hit man), who told Mark that, under orders, he had kidnapped Walter Winchell and was under instructions to "waste" him. The Mob had learned that Winchell had been given some information that would, if printed, put the finger on several upper-echelon hoodlums. Winchell, at gunpoint, promised to forget the whole thing, but Coll had no reason to believe that promise. Winchell pleaded: "If Hellinger vouches for my silence, would you reconsider?" Coll called Mark; Mark met with him and Winchell and gave his (and Winchell's) word that the story would be forgotten. Coll phoned his bosses and put Hellinger on the phone and he repeated his promise. Winchell was released; the story never broke. Mark never told what had happened, and no one ever knew about it until a Mafia chief, years later, made a plea bargain and included the events of that night. Winchell didn't have too many friends—but Hellinger was at the top of the list.

Mark was just about the most loyal person around. He was also, no contest, the heaviest and best drinker in the world. He could put away a bottle of brandy at a sitting and never show a trace of it. Dowling and I were once with him at another famous watering hole —Dinty Moore's—when a pale and poorly dressed patron approached and asked if he was talking to Mark Hellinger. He was. He introduced himself as a very recently released prisoner from Sing Sing who had boasted to his cronies that he was able to drink anyone under the table. They had told him to look up Mark Hellinger and report back to them on visiting day. Mark simply said, "Let's find out." Hellinger ordered a bottle of brandy, his challenger ordered a bottle of bourbon, and the four of us moved to a back table. The rules were: a two-hour time limit, no food, and no mixers. Each poured and the contest began. An hour later each man had finished two bottles. Mark was about to order two more when his opponent stood up, not steadily, shook hands, and said, "Mr. Hellinger, I know when I'm beat. You are in a class by yourself and me, I've got a report to make. I hope you'll allow me to pay for the drinks." That was the only time I know of that Mark let someone pick up the tab.

Hellinger eventually went to Hollywood, became a respected writer/producer of such movies as *The Killers* and *The Horn Blows at Midnight,* and was as beloved there as in New York. When he died, in his early forties, the cause was "something about his liver." I lost a dear friend. So did a lot of people. And a few distillers.

This may be the proper place for me to interject a story about a personal meeting with a member of the underworld. As a stage manager at the Winter Garden, I was attracted to a young blonde chorus girl who was always pleasant and polite to me but a little bit distant. I hoped that as time passed she might become more impressed with me, but the best I could do was walk her from the Garden to her second, late-night job at the Paradise Café, where we'd have a drink at the bar and she'd thank me and hurry backstage.

On the fourth or fifth of these occasions, Peggy said the usual good night and went to her dressing room and I started to leave. The maitre d' stopped me and asked me to follow him. I did and was led to a ringside table occupied by three dark-suited, unsmiling, very sharp-looking men. They asked me to sit and join them —there were some questions they wanted to ask me. Such as:

"Is your name Fred?"

"That's right."

"Do you know a girl named Peggy?"

"Yes. I do."

"Does she work at the Winter Garden?"

"Yeah. Why?"

"I'll explain later. Are you something like her boyfriend?"

"Not really. I just like her."

"That's all, huh!"

"Right."

"Well, that's real lucky for you. You see, she and I have a kind of relationship where I pay her rent and buy her clothes. And if you were to get too close to her, my friend Mr. Colt wouldn't like it at all."

He lifted his napkin from his plate and exposed

"Mr. Colt," a very deadly looking revolver. Peggy and I didn't spend much time together after that.

A major difference between New York and Hollywood is the work schedule—and the play schedule. In the West you arrive on the set in the morning, finish shooting in the evening, and arrange your fun time so that you are home early enough to repeat the operation the next day. In my New York era, mornings were for sleeping, theater time was from eight till eleven-thirty at night, and at midnight the social season opened.

Sherman Billingsley ran a famous night spot called the Stork Club. John Perona owned an even more elegant watering hole—El Morocco. Just about every night the Shubert foursome was in attendance at one or the other—not necessarily in a group or at one time —with or without a date, each of us knowing that there would be an open chair upon arrival. From the start, there was a formula for paying the evening checks: Shubert paid fifty percent, Dowling and Cohen each paid twenty percent, and, as a newcomer, I was in for the remaining ten percent. As salaries shifted so did the formula. I remember a reunion during the early days of World War II: Shubert and Dowling were in the army, Cohen was in the navy, and I was directing at Warner Bros. Johnny revised the formula for the last time—one percent each if you were in the Armed Forces and ninety-seven percent if you were working in Hollywood.

Dowling and Cohen lived in apartments; Johnny had a large suite at the Astor and arranged for me to have a nice-enough single room there too. I'm stunned nowadays when a New York hotel breakfast costs twenty dollars—I paid three dollars a day for that room at the Astor.

Whenever J. J. Shubert left on a European vacation, however, there was an abrupt change in our accommodations. J.J. always traveled by ocean liner, visited his London and Paris offices, then rested up by taking the mineral baths in Germany—each vacation lasted four weeks. By the time his boat had cleared the Statue of Liberty, four elated young men were the occupants of that great penthouse atop the Sardi Building, eating the finest foods, drinking the best wines, and entertaining the combined chorus lines of all the Shubert musicals. We all wished Mr. J.J. happy —and numerous—vacations.

Even though Johnny eventually married a charming chorus girl from *The Show Is On,* Eddie and Abe remained single and I didn't get married to Janet—or anyone else—till I was fifty-three years old. From 1933 to 1943 the four of us remained close friends and constant companions. Later all three visited me when they came to California, and I them when I went East.

There was one substantial change, however, and I'm not sure I can explain it. While apparently a happily married man, Johnny married another young lady —in Florida—in addition. No one was aware of the situation until Mrs. Shubert II sent announcements of the birth of a son to everyone in his address book— including Mrs. Shubert I. I was glad to be three thousand miles away when that news hit the fan.

On, and Very Often
Far From, Broadway

From 1933 through 1943 I was, as a Shubert Fred-of-all-trades, a gofer, a stage manager, a director, and a producer. It wasn't exactly a period of my life during which I chose exactly on what and with whom I wanted to work. It was a period during which I did what I was told to do. And what I did wasn't always successful, but it was exciting and it was fun.

In these days producers and directors and performers take years to agree upon the proper script, the right theater, and whether they can arrange their schedules to work together in the foreseeable future. In my days I would function as the stage manager of a revue at the Winter Garden, as director of a road company of *The Student Prince* or *Blossom Time,* put a light comedy into rehearsal until a ''name'' director agreed to contract terms, replace a ''name'' director who proved to be a director in name only, produce Shubert Summer Operettas seasons in Kentucky or Tennessee or Canada—changing the venue and my status all year long and at a minute's notice. I learned to keep my suitcase packed.

The stars were famous, the opening nights were exciting, and long before that unfortunate skier in the Wide World of Sports, there was the "thrill of victory and the agony of defeat." There were romances of varying length and intensity; and there were the non-stop rehearsals and rewrites when a show was on the road "pre-Broadway." There was the sadness of closing a show before it ever had the chance to open in New York, and the excitement of opening-night parties with the endless waiting until the first edition of the *Times* let you know if you were a hit or a miss. There was the first theater program where my name appeared in tiny print as the stage manager, and the first time I read my name in bold letters, "entire production staged and directed by." Everything seemed so important at the time, but some of my clearest memories are of people and events of no major impact but wonderful to think back on.

For instance, my most memorable romance was with a petite, beautiful, extremely "experienced" French actress—Simone Simon. She had achieved some success in her homeland and had been brought to Hollywood, where she became considerably more famous for her boudoir activities than for her appearances on the screen. Lee Shubert found her perfectly suited to star in a musical, *Three After Three* (music and lyrics by Hoagy Carmichael and Johnny Mercer), and to New York she came. She and the assigned director quickly discovered that their personas were in sharp conflict, and I was assigned to replace him. My persona fit perfectly with Simone's.

Eighteen remarkable weeks ensued: four weeks of rehearsal and fourteen weeks in Baltimore, Boston, Philadelphia, Pittsburgh, Chicago, Cincinnati, and Detroit, getting the show ready for Broadway. There was great frustration onstage but total gratification otherwise. I hoped the rewriting and revamping would take

Simone Simon caused me to smile a lot.

forever. My directorial career may have been at a standstill, but "love was sweeping the country." Eventually, Mr. Lee tired of losing sizable sums each week, posted the closing notice, and *Three After Three* folded. Cast and crew returned to New York and resumed their pre-show lives. Unfortunately, Simone's pre-show life revolved around a longtime admirer, Raymond Hakim, who gently told me at Pennsylvania Station that Simone had "spoken very highly" of me and he hoped I'd find time to have dinner with them before they sailed for France. I was heartbroken, but it was my own fault—I had forgotten the show-business axiom: "They were madly in love, but the show closed." Simone and I haven't seen each other often over the years, but I'm always delighted to receive her Christmas cards addressed to Mr. and

Mrs. Fred de Cordova—and a hand-written notation: "With happy memories." I have them, too.

Less intense was a dalliance with an actress of some standing who shared a town house with the brilliant writer and wit Dorothy Parker. I had often read of Miss Parker's penetrating humor and sharp tongue. During my tenure, Miss Parker's witticisms were confined to such pungent comments as "My, isn't the weather dreadful!" and "I'm on my way to dinner, enjoy yourselves." There's a happy ending. Some weeks later at "21," I escorted a perennially unsuccessful ingenue to dinner and passed Miss Parker's table. I introduced them, and Dorothy asked the young lady if it was true that she was about to sign a movie contract. "No," said the ingenue, "I'm afraid I'm wedded to the theater." Miss Parker answered, "If I were you, I would sue it for nonsupport." It was worth the wait.

Prince Michael Romanoff (or Harry Gurgeson, a Brooklyn tailor) fooled a lot of people for a long time. Charming and beautifully mannered, he claimed to be the sole surviving heir to the Crown of Russia. But since the Revolution had cut off his funds, he found it necessary to work for a living. One of his "temporary" employments was as a "greeter" at several posh nightclubs. He knew most of the customers by name, was courteous to all, and had "the power of the pencil"—which means he was empowered by the management to buy, and sign for, drinks for regular patrons. Whether or not he was a true Romanoff wasn't so important—everyone liked him.

One night I was waiting at the bar for some friends to arrive when Prince Mike took me aside, apologized for intruding, and explained he was suffering a temporary financial problem. He would be extremely grateful if I could spare him fifty dollars for a few days. I was able to help out. Before the evening ended he pressed a small packet into my hand "as security for the loan," in case something should happen to him. At home, I examined the "security"—a pair of obviously dime-store cuff links.

Several days later we met again, and he returned the loan. I was pleased to get my money back—and a bit surprised. Even more so when he reminded me that I had in my possession a pair of "heirloom" cuff links that he had given to me. "When you have the opportunity, please return them."

Anyone that brassy and classy deserved to open and run for many years one of Beverly Hills' most exclusive and successful restaurants. Romanoff's was one of the really "in" places, Mike was most careful of the selection of his customers because "he couldn't abide phonies." Until his death he insisted that the Communist conspiracy kept him from being the czar of all the Russias.

It is always a thrill to be a discoverer, to be there at the beginning. Two Shubert-days "finds" rank high on my all-time list. The first reaped quite a harvest. Mr. Lee Shubert was told that a young producer/director had assembled a batch of talented young performers and had put together a very amusing show playing at a resort hotel in the Catskill Mountains. He thought I should check the show out and report if there was anyone in it who might be of value to the firm. Let's just say that there sure as hell was. Among the performers were Danny Kaye, Sylvia Fine, Imogene Coca, Alfred Drake, and Jerome Robbins. I raved to Mr. Lee, who drove up to see it the next night and struck a deal immediately, and the *Straw Hat Revue* opened three months later at the Ambassador Theater. The critics enjoyed it, and everyone in it went on to considerable success. To jog your memory: Danny Kaye married Sylvia Fine, and Sam Goldwyn starred him, and her songs, in one movie hit after another; Max Liebman, the producer/director, invented one of television's gems—*Your Show of Shows,* co-starring Sid Caesar and Miss Coca; Alfred Drake captured audiences as Curly in *Oklahoma*; and Jerry Robbins ranks as one of the country's top choreographers. It was a worthwhile trip to the Catskills.

Another treasure was discovered one night on Fifty-second Street. Johnny Shubert and I had dinner at "21," spent an hour or two next door at Leon and Eddie's nightclub, where Ella Logan and Martha Raye sang some great saloon songs, and decided to have a nightcap across the street at Jack White's "18 Club." This club featured the comic Mr. White, another funny man, Pat Harrington, Sr., and anyone they came up with who could contribute to their unscripted and unrehearsed craziness. The night we dropped in, the added starter was a handsome, heavyset, part-time musician and always funny man—Jackie Gleason. The Shuberts were producing and I was scheduled to direct a new musical, *Keep Off the Grass*. Mr. Gleason generated a lot of laughs that night, was engaged to join Jimmy Durante and Ray Bolger in *Grass,* and the country "honeymooned" and "cannonballed" with him ever after.

Then there were the two other fellows I bumped into along the way. One of them was the "world's greatest entertainer." That must have been the truth, because his business card stated simply: "Al Jolson, World's Greatest Entertainer." He wasn't exactly adored by his co-workers, but his card didn't say he was adorable, just the greatest. I stage-managed when he starred in the town's hottest ticket—the Sunday Night Concerts at the Winter Garden. The best available vaudeville stars were booked to make up Act One. Mr. Jolson, working on a runway that extended far into the audience, was Act Two. It had to be that way—no one could follow him. You've seen his life portrayed in pictures, you know he changed movie history when he did *The Jazz Singer* and sounded the death knell of silent pictures; but, as they say, you had to be there when he halted the applause, said "You ain't heard nothing yet," and started to hum the first few bars of "Swanee."

There's a Jolson anecdote about the first time he said "You ain't heard nothing yet"—my elders swear it's true. It happened during a star-studded benefit for the sale of war bonds in World War I. George M. Cohan had just written what became the theme song of that war—"Over There." He sang it for the first time that night, and the audience cheered. A little later in the program, Enrico Caruso performed several arias and finished his "turn" by saying that Mr. Cohan had written a sensational song and he would like to present his version. He did "Over There" to a standing ovation. The closing performer of the evening was Mr. Jolson. He sang for twenty minutes and was, as always, a smash hit. He said the audience had heard music history that night when Mr. Cohan and Mr. Caruso performed a magnificent new song. "But," he added, "sit in your seats and open your ears, because I promise you, you ain't heard nothing yet." He sang a chorus of "Over There," Cohan and Caruso joined him onstage, and they all sang the song together. I wish I'd been there and I bet you do, too.

Great star that he was, Jolson was as insecure as he was talented. Several times I was in his dressing room at the Garden when he turned the faucets in his washbasin on full force so he couldn't hear the applause for the other performers.

Never quite as big a star as Jolson but a huge success nonetheless, was another outstanding singer, Harry Richman. Among the hits he introduced were "Birth of the Blues," "This Is My Lucky Day," "Put-

Harry Richman: the "Birth of the Blues" man.

tin' on the Ritz," "Stay As Sweet As You Are," and "Walking My Baby Back Home." He started as Mae West's piano accompanist, became a vaudeville headliner, starred in many *George White Scandals,* opened his own "formal-attire-only" nightclub—the Club Richman—and was as charming offstage as on. He was equally at ease with Al Capone as with the Prince of Wales. I never worked with him when he was at the very top. He made a fortune and spent two. Overgenerous as he was, there came a time when booze and overwork took his great voice away, and the offers became fewer and then stopped completely. During his last years, three or four of us combined to ease his financial woes, and just before he packed it in, he transferred every record he'd ever made onto tape and sent the package to me with this note enclosed:

Dear Pal Fred,
   If ever you're feeling a little blue and I'm not around to cheer you up, please play a few of these tunes. Richman will be doing his show from the Sky Room, and the performance is dedicated to you.

Stay as sweet as you are.
Harry

You may have to jog your memory a bit to recall the beautiful and outrageous Tallulah Bankhead. She hasn't been with us for some time, but when she was in action—she certainly was. Spending time with her wasn't exactly like attending a meeting of the Holy Name Society.

Well educated but never housebroken, she spoke several languages fluently and sprinkled them liberally with all the well-known four-letter words and a few she invented and helped to make popular.

England adopted her as its favorite stage star; she was a Broadway sensation in Lillian Hellman's *Little Foxes*; her screen career peaked in Alfred Hitchcock's *Lifeboat*; and the aptly named *Tallulah Bankhead Show* was a sizable success on the air.

I first met her in my New York nightclub days, admired her talent and beauty, her picturesque choice of words, her ability to drink along with the boys, and her surprising expertise in the world of big-league baseball. She was a rabid fan of the (then) New York Giants, and once, when they were in a slump, gave up liquor until they won a game. It was a prolonged slump —a blow to their supporters and the distillers of the world.

Tallulah Bankhead, who made late night exciting—even before Johnny Carson entered my life.

Tallulah and I spent many evenings at the Stork Club, often proceeded uptown to the Harlem late spots, and sometimes wound up for a nightcap at her suite in the Gotham Hotel. On one eventful occasion I felt that the moment had arrived to move from friendship to something more. Talloo appeared to understand my feeling, seemed to approve of the prospect, but explained she had to work on some new scenes for an upcoming play. I remember vividly how she solved the situation:

"Fred dahling, why don't you hop into bed, I'll send my maid in to get things started, and as soon as I've done my work, I'll join you all."

That night I learned that "you all" was something more than a Southern expression.

Her co-star in *Lifeboat,* Hume Cronyn, an extremely gifted actor, director, and raconteur, adds another footnote to the Bankhead legend:

The lifeboat, in which most of the picture's action took place, was elevated high off the sound stage's floor so that it could be rocked in any direction, thereby simulating the action of the sea.

The performers had to climb a ladder in order to reach their places in the boat.

As the star of the picture, Tallulah climbed the ladder first. However, she had no tolerance for the use of undergarments; she felt they were unnecessary and constricting. The other actors followed her up the ladder, and the consensus was that the view was a hazard not called for in the script. They went to Mr. Hitchcock and explained the problem they faced.

But the famous director demurred, saying that he had been hired to direct the performances of the actors and felt that the grievance might better be solved by (a) the wardrobe department, (b) the makeup department, or (c) hairdressing.

Add a final Bankhead story, which could well be apocryphal, although she was willing to claim it was true. A rich and attractive admirer was smitten enough to put his arms around Tallulah and say, "I want you for my wife." The answer: "That's very flattering, dahling, but I don't even know your wife."

Ted Husing was the Vin Scully of his day—simply the best sports announcer in the business. He loved backstage life—and a lot of girls who worked there. I identified with his interests, and we spent a lot of time together. He was a tireless worker, an expert in sports history, and probably the best-prepared sportscaster ever. Here's an example: The night before the famous horse race—the Belmont Stakes—was to be run (he had been assigned to "call it"), I sat in his apartment and watched him place sixteen pieces of paper in a top hat, each the color of a jockey's silks. He'd reach into the hat, pick out one of the papers after another, and announce—as if the race were in progress—who was leading, who was second, and on through the order of finish. He'd then repeat the process until he was completely secure that he would be able, the next day, to identify the horse and the jockey when the race was run. Finally, he decided to pour us a nightcap and do it one more time. While he mixed the drinks, I pocketed one of the slips of paper. He returned and called the race as if he were on the air—announced the results of the imaginary race, what jockeys were "up," and then turned to me, exclaiming, "This race is about to be protested. A hoax has been perpetrated on the American public. Some son of a bitch has stolen Alfred Vanderbilt's horse." The next day we went to Belmont Park, and the Stakes was won by a horse and jockey sporting the cerise-and-white diamonds of Alfred Gwynne Vanderbilt. I could have called the winner—I had the proper slip of paper in my pocket.

Not too long ago Francis Albert Sinatra, John William Carson, and I were sitting at Chasen's bar waiting for our Flame martinis. They were discussing the possibility, and the fun it might be, of appearing together in a two-man show at Radio City Music Hall. I was there primarily because I was the host.

Pepe served us his specialty and said they were on the house in memory of the good old days. That comment started a long and pleasant evening devoted to our memories of people and places—some good and some not so. On balance, I look back with pleasure.

I first met Bob Hope in my early Shubert days. In 1936 he was starring at the Winter Garden, along with

Two rather well-known comics aren't overly impressed with my directorial suggestions.

Fanny Brice and Josephine Baker, in *The Follies*. I was the stage manager. It was in that musical that he sang "I Can't Get Started with You" to Eve Arden while Bunny Berrigan played his trumpet accompaniment in the pit band. Since then I've directed him in television specials, the movie *I'll Take Sweden,* and enjoyed dozens of his appearances on *The Tonight Show*. There's no other phrase but "he's amazing" that aptly fits Bob Hope. On a personal note, we both find it almost impossible to believe we started our friendship and our golf matches over fifty years ago.

In that same vein, it was almost that long ago when I was backstage on the opening night when Larry Hagman's mother sang "My Heart Belongs to Daddy" and in one night became the talk of the town. Mary Martin was a lovely girl back then—she's a lovely lady now.

Jimmy Durante listens to Jackie Gleason—long before "The Honeymooners."

Jack Buchanan, London's number-one musical star (directed by me in *Between the Devil*; I bet you still remember *I'll Go Way by Myself* and *Triplets*), gave me two bits of sage advice: (1) always pour a few drops of vinegar on oysters; and (2) never wear underpants—they are demeaning when it is important for you to look your best. I pointed out that at other times it could be a concern. He quoted Winston Churchill: "A dead bird never falls from a nest."

Otto Preminger was directing a play (*Beverly Hills*) for the Shuberts. Mr. Lee Shubert was less than delighted with Otto's efforts and dispatched me to discuss the situation with him. I tried, politely, to indicate that the head man felt what he had seen at rehearsals left something to be desired. Instead of taking umbrage and turning in his uniform (as was expected), Mr. Preminger agreed he had made some casting errors, thought I would be the perfect person to play the Young Policeman, fired the incumbent, and hired me. The critics saved all of us from too long a period of shame.

Mike Todd, presumably the most prolific spender of them all, once lost an acceptable amount of money to me in a card game. And didn't pay. We played a while later, he lost again, and again he didn't pay. A mutual friend suggested that we meet a third time. Mike declined, saying, "No way. If you lose three times in a row, you have to pay." When he died in a plane crash, the world lost a remarkable, flamboyant gentleman. I still miss him—and I miss that third game.

I worked as Jimmy Durante's director on *Keep Off the Grass* and we became close friends. So close that he told me who Mrs. Calabash actually was—but made me promise never to tell anyone else. So I won't. But, "Good night, Mrs. Calabash, wherever you are"—and thanks for your friendship, Jimmy.

There were challenging career moments with a young Milton Berle, Fanny Brice, and Ray Bolger and Bert Lahr (long before they became the Scarecrow and the Cowardly Lion), and I had the foresight as their "director" to stand mute and nod while Olsen and Johnson directed themselves in *Hellzapoppin'*.

But I guess the highlight was working twice with the theater's number-one comedienne, Beatrice Lillie. I stage-managed the first time, and some years later, she requested me as a director. She was the titled Lady Peel in private life and a brilliant hoyden onstage. She was also the first star I know of who presented gifts—substantial ones—to her co-workers *before* opening night. She explained that the critics were liable to make our friendships short-lived, so the gifts could be for opening night and, also, farewell.

Finally, New York-wise, I directed Milton Berle

Milton Berle, Ilona Massey and Arthur Treacher starred in the 1942 *Ziegfeld Follies*—my last Broadway musical.

Beatrice Lillie (Lady Peel) shares a table (and drinks) with Reggie Gardiner, my mother, a certain young director and Eddie Dowling, after a performance of *At Home Abroad*.

"Baby Snooks" (Fanny Brice)—the funniest lady on Broadway. I was her stage manager in the *Ziegfeld Follies* of 1935.

and Ilona Massey and Arthur Treacher in a very well-received *Ziegfeld Follies,* and Hollywood made me some most welcome offers. I chose Warner Bros. over MGM, although the salary was about the same, because Bette Davis and Barbara Stanwyck and Ann Sheridan were under contract to Warner's—and a man could dream, couldn't he?

Pepe's comment about the good old days sparked a lively conversation among Carson, Sinatra, and me about the general belief that Then rather than Now was when we had the most fun and that the places we went and the people we knew a while back were more exciting and interesting than they are today.

I remembered a remark attributed to Don Juan. When asked who of all the women he had bedded had been the most memorable, he is said to have replied that it was most likely the first, because it would have been a new and enchanting experience; but, on second thought, it must have been the most recent, because it is the freshest in the memory; then again, chances are it was some lovely in between—after all, how nice it is that there have been so many to choose from. I feel much the same when I try to evaluate which period of my life is my favorite. We've touched on Broadway. Let's move West and discuss the Movie Years.

Hollywood—the Place
and the People

When I arrived in Hollywood a million years ago, in many respects it was a completely different place than it is today. Beverly Hills was a small town, Sunset Boulevard was bisected by a bridle path, South Rodeo Drive was just another street for convenience shopping in moderately priced stores set between pleasant-enough one-story homes. The Beverly Hills Hotel and the Beverly Wilshire Hotel were in existence, but the Bel Air Hotel was still a stable. There was a miniature golf course on Wilshire Boulevard directly opposite the Beverly Wilshire Hotel, and a real golf course where the Twentieth Century-Fox back lot, with its French and German and Italian and New York streets, had been erected to make location shooting unnecessary.

Westwood was a charming college town. The Big Red Line of streetcars took passengers from downtown Los Angeles all the way to Santa Monica and the Pacific Ocean for a twenty-five cent fare, and Ventura Boulevard was framed by citrus groves instead of lighting-fixture stores.

Downtown Hollywood featured Grauman's Chinese and Egyptian picture palaces; Warner's and Paramount built their movie flagships nearby. Rich native Californians lived in beautiful homes on and around Rossmore Avenue, and those homes actually had space between them.

Hollywood meant motion pictures, Pasadena meant retirement in luxury, Palm Springs was a small desert town primarily owned by Indians, Malibu was for ocean lovers who didn't care if they had neighbors or not, the inhabitants of the area were not "blessed" by freeways, almost all travel to the East was by train and to Hawaii and the Orient by ocean liner.

There was no such thing as television, most domestic help was Japanese, not Mexican (some folks tended their own gardens), oil companies and the movie studios were the hub of community interest. But one thing was the same: the homes of the rich and the famous were in Beverly Hills.

And one other thing was the same: the studio walls were high, but the walls of society were even higher. It was quickly clear to me that The Men were the powers in the movie industry but even clearer that The Wives held the power over The Men who were the powers.

Let's assume that you came to town, as I did, during the "glory years," when a few special ladies determined the social status of a newcomer. Let's also assume you recognized that social acceptance was, in some cases, even more valuable to a career than talent. The chances are you'd realize that it was an advantage to "be a member."

During my New York years some of my close friends had received the call to California. By the time I showed up on the scene they were established in some prestigious positions: Hellinger was a prominent producer; Jack and Mary Benny had moved West for movie-making and television; *New York Mirror* columnist Jerry Wald was a major writer/producer; Fanny Brice was an MGM star; Gene Kelly was already at the top; so was Van Heflin (who played the Jimmy Stewart part onstage in *The Philadelphia Story*); not to mention the most remarkable of them all—Cary Grant. They each had a shot at forgetting they had known me in the past and they didn't take it. On the contrary.

Rather quickly I found myself an accepted "escort." Translation: an extra man who knows better than to suggest he be permitted to bring along a girl of his choice. Instead he will pick up and drive home (no matter how far away she lives) a grieving widow or a chronically tipsy character actress or a charming beauty whose husband is working late but will arrive "after dinner" to make sure that no other man hears the words that hooked him originally: "Wouldn't you like to come in for a nightcap?"

Yes indeed, even before you can say Robin Leach, there I was in the homes of the rich and famous. The nights were varied, just as yours are when you are on the town: some were outstanding, some you thought would never end, and there were some when you made a fool of yourself. Join me as I experienced each of the above at the dinner tables of:

> The David Selznicks
> The Ronald Colmans
> The Samuel Goldwyns
> The William Goetzes
> The Jack Warners
> The Charles Lederers
> The Jack Bennys
> Sam Spiegel
> The Harry Cohns
> The James Masons

If you're not exactly sure just who these folks are, or were, it is only fair that I bring them sharply into focus.

Irene and David Selznick

Not then, and not now, was there a more coveted invitation than: "The David Selznicks hope you'll be able to join them for cocktails on——." David, the producer of *Gone With the Wind, Duel in the Sun, Rebecca,* and *The Paradine Case,* among others, was one of the two (we'll get to Sam Goldwyn shortly) most respected producers in the industry. His father, Lewis Selznick, one of the true motion-picture pioneers, took on some of his confreres (Louis B. Mayer, Joseph Schenck, Thomas Ince, and Adolph Zukor, let's say), and in doing so, wound up broke and broken. David and his brother, Myron, never forgot. Myron became the most feared agent in town, used his clients as pawns as he played one studio against another, and delighted in extracting the last drop of available financial blood from "the enemy." David, on the other hand, joined the studio world until he made a towering name for himself and then went independent and broke all the gentleman's agreements the cartel had set up to protect themselves. And wallowed happily in the consternation he caused.

Naturally David married a woman who shared his rebellious attitude—a woman who felt the same disdain for the Establishment that he did. Well, not exactly. His bride was the daughter of Louis B. Mayer of, you guessed it, Metro-Goldwyn-Mayer. Irene, along with David, created a social salon comprised of the brightest minds, the wittiest conversationalists, and the most iconoclastic thinkers west of New York's Algonquin Hotel. Food and wine were first quality, as was the after-dinner entertainment, furnished by the guests. Long before Trivial Pursuit reared its irritating head, there was the "you-better-have-an-amusing-answer-or-feel-like-a-dunce" series of Selznick-invented word games. By the time you headed home, you had assimilated enough smart talk to shine in your less spectacular circles and you could pretend you'd thought of all those amusing comments yourself. My moment of acceptance as a member arrived when in answer to David's question: "What is MGM's most successful song?" I answered: "By Mayer Bist Du Schoen." On second thought, maybe it wasn't such a sophisticated group!

David still is the record holder as the most prolific note writer in movie history. He supervised every facet of his productions, and every employee received daily written "suggestions" (many eight to ten pages in length) covering such areas as an immediate change in the color of the blanket rolls on Gregory Peck's horse, to the exact time of the day when a certain scene was to be shot (no matter how long the company had to stand by till that time arrived), and including day-by-day reminders not to shoot close-ups of leading ladies during their menstrual cycle—"schedule is attached." Clearly David was a detail man.

When his marriage to Irene fell apart, she shifted her headquarters to New York and became a major success as a Broadway producer—*A Streetcar Named Desire,* for instance. David eventually married a stunning young actress named Jennifer Jones, who, after David's death, married multimillionaire Norton Simon. Looking back, everyone did rather well.

Benita and Ronald Colman

You just couldn't create a more handsome man and a more attractive woman. The Colmans were the established and acknowledged leaders of the English Set —and we know how inferior the English make all of us feel. Ronnie's tremendous success as an actor and Benita's built-in worldliness made their home just about the hottest ticket in town. Not exactly a Britisher, I managed to gain my entry through a young British actress with whom I spent a number of lovely evenings. Currently married to Joseph Cotten, Patricia Medina, then and now an absolute stunner, broke most of the accepted rules by having, in addition to beauty, a Top Ten sense of humor.

Before my first evening at the Colmans' Pat gave me gentle but specific instructions on how to behave: I was not to move in too quickly, it was not necessary for me to be the designated storyteller, and it might be wise to take my conduct cues from the David Nivenses, the Doug Fairbanks, Juniors, and the William Powells (all Colman regulars). I listened and acted accordingly. During the cocktail hour I confined myself to the obviously acceptable arenas of politeness and flattery. I had, of course, seen all of Mr. Colman's movies and discussed them in detail. He seemed pleased, and a nod from Pat indicated I was passing muster. At dinner Niven mentioned he had seen and liked a picture I had directed, and I was both pleased and uncharacteristically humble. All was going well— until I saw that the butler was preparing to pour a vintage red wine. Explaining that wine gave me a headache, I turned my wineglass over so that I wouldn't be served—and discovered that my glass had already been filled. As the red stain spread . . .

Ronald Colman: you want to talk handsome!

and spread . . . and spread over the linen, Colman turned to Pat and, in his world-famous voice, asked: "Pat, what did you say his name was?"

In spite of, or maybe because of, my gaffe, the Colmans became very close friends of mine. We spent many happy evenings together, and when Ronnie sold the big house and they moved to their ranch in Santa Barbara, he sent me a case of his favorite red wine with a message: "Enjoy. This is equally acceptable for drinking or spilling."

Frances and Sam Goldwyn

Sam was a Goldfish before he was a Goldwyn. Someone wisely decided that Metro-Goldwyn-Mayer sounded and looked better than Metro-Goldfish-Mayer. He had been a successful glove salesman, clearly a natural stepping-stone to producing motion pictures, but, as the head of the Goldwyn Studios, he was responsible for some of the most successful and tasteful pictures ever to reach the screen—*Wuthering Heights, The Best Years of Our Lives,* and *Stella Dallas,* among others. But he became most famous for his long list of malapropisms: "An oral agreement isn't worth the paper it's written on"; "I'll give you my answer in two words, 'im possible' "; and one instruction he gave to me—"I'll thank you to look at me when I'm listening to you."

Sam was almost as famous for his explosive temper. One night, in a gin game, the cards ran against him and he was blitzed (at sizable stakes) six games in a row. He threw his cards in the air, rose from the card table, stormed out of the card room, through the living room, to the front door. There he stopped, turned to his stunned opponents, and stated that he would never play cards "in this house again." He exited, slamming the door. After a considerable pause, he returned—having finally realized that the card game had been in his own home.

Frances, a former actress and a beauty, was a soothing influence on his life and the lives of his many friends. Of more importance, she was the first hostess to ask me if I'd like to bring a date of my own choice. Talk about a breakthrough!

Edie and Bill Goetz

William Goetz, another force in the movie industry, was at various times the head man of Twentieth Century-Fox and Universal-International. A shrewd businessman and an experienced moviemaker, he married still another daughter of L. B. Mayer. Edie (Mayer Goetz) and Irene (Mayer Selznick) were friendly rivals in marriages, dinner parties, house staffs, wardrobes, art acquisitions, and prestige. On second thought, maybe the rivalry wasn't so friendly. On third thought, maybe they didn't really like each other at all. Edie, totally secure in her belief that she was the reigning queen of the town, attending a gala given by a social pretender (no, not Irene), viewing the lavish buffet, the marimba orchestra, and the extravagant table decorations, turned to Bill and quietly stated her position: "Darling, why do they try?"

Billy Goetz may well have been the most amusing executive of them all. Certainly he was the most happy with his life-style and his life itself. And he delighted everyone with his completely irreverent sense of humor. Example one: At the funeral of a major studio figure, he realized that Jeanette MacDonald was about to pay, vocally, a sad and fond farewell. Just before her first solemn note, he turned to me and whispered, "When she starts to sing, make very sure that you don't laugh." She began her song, and I damn near joined the corpse. Example two: At a dinner party a group was doing a deserved hatchet job on a pushy, self-satisfied newcomer to the community. As "the subject" came into view, Bill beckoned her to join the group. She did. Bill told her: "Your ears must be burning . . . everyone here has been talking about you." He then turned to the number-one put-downer and continued: "Why don't you tell our newfound friend all the nice things you were just saying about her," and walked away.

Ann and Jack Warner

It was often said that Jack Warner would rather tell a bad joke than make a good picture. He made a lot of both. I worked for him for five years, respected his movie savvy, disliked his utter ruthlessness, but generally found him fascinating. Ann was a true beauty, warm and outgoing—and Jack was very jealous. I was one of a number of young men who, at Warner gatherings, found it wiser to be ignored than adored. To be place-carded next to Mrs. Warner and to be complimented by her caused immediate and severe indigestion. Rolaids, industrial strength, couldn't blunt Jack's piercing glances. Although totally innocent, both in mind and in body, I still found Warner nights extremely uncomfortable. The day he fired me—to show, I guess, that it was only because of my lack of talent, not my lack of charm—he invited me to dinner. I accepted, and for the first time was unconcerned when Ann embraced me and said, "Jack, I'm so glad you invited my favorite boyfriend." After all, if you've already been fired, you don't have too much to worry about.

Warner, in general, always treated me as a son

rather than as an employee. On the other hand, he treated his son as an employee and finally barred him from entering the studio grounds. Jack, Jr., wasn't the only one barred. Jesse Lasky (an industry pioneer and a respected producer under contract to Warner) was given a studio lunch in the executive dining bungalow just before he was to leave for a European vacation. Jack toasted him on his accomplishments and as a valued friend and wished him a happy holiday. Lasky drove home after the tribute, discovered he had left some needed addresses at the studio, returned a few hours later—and found himself prohibited from entering the premises and told his belongings would be sent to his home "as soon as your office has been cleaned out." Happy Holiday!

Several years after I was terminated at the studio, I ran into Mr. W. at a dinner party. He told me that, over the years, he had hired a lot of people and made a lot of mistakes—and that he'd fired a lot of people and never made a mistake. I guess I fell into both categories.

It's my assumption that Jack Warner wasn't an out-and-out ogre but, rather, a product of his times.

Annie and Charles Lederer

Anne Shirley, a pretty, vivacious, less-than-major star, and her husband, Charley Lederer (Marion Davies's nephew and a valued collaborator of top writers Ben Hecht and Charles MacArthur), gave wonderful New Year's Eve parties. They were huge affairs with tents, alternating orchestras, unlimited caviar, all-nighters. They also gave many smaller, more conversational get-togethers—very star-oriented and equally posh. At one of these, Anne, who knew of my long-standing crush on Marlene Dietrich, was darling enough to place-card me on Miss Dietrich's right. I was in eighth heaven. During the evening I made every possible effort to enchant her: I stressed my admiration for her as a talent and my recognition of her beauty; I knew the date of her upcoming opening in Las Vegas and was clearing my schedule so that I could be in attendance; I even spoke German to her. Nothing worked! At all! All my "charm" brought nothing but one-word answers, followed by silence. Eventually I recognized defeat and reluctantly turned my attentions elsewhere. But I remained ready for a change in attitude and alert for one more attempt. It came. I saw that Miss Dietrich was about to smoke a cigarette. Quickly I struck a match, turned to the lovely lady, and lit the cigarette. Only it wasn't a cigarette, it was a marabou powder puff—which flared wildly, scorched her nose, and sent her flying from the room. In a sense, I had managed to get her attention.

Mary and Jack Benny

Mary and Jack. I still can't write their names without a great sense of loss. They were my primary sponsors in Tinsel Town, as well as my closest friends. I first knew them in my New York days. I was directing a musical, *High Kickers,* starring George Jessel and Sophie Tucker, and the Bennys came backstage to visit their friends, Georgie and Soph. They invited me to join them for supper at El Morocco—and the closeness never stopped until I gave the eulogies at both their funerals. No, it still hasn't stopped. We worked together, played golf and cards together, Palm Springed and Europed together, and when we were apart we were on the phone a lot. The Bennys and the de Cordovas were a happy foursome. Both Mary and Jack loved Janet, and she misses them as much as I

My favorite picture with my favorite man—Jack Benny.
I still miss him.

do . . . maybe more. No matter how many people you
meet as time goes by, you just can't replace the ones
who were so close for so long.

I've mentioned that Jack, as opposed to his screen
image, was just about the most generous man in the
world. He enjoyed buying "for-no-reason" gifts for
his pals and his family, and it's a good thing he felt
that way himself, because Mary earned her black belt
in spending. To this day, I don't think anyone has
topped her record. Jewelry, clothes, whatever—she
was the champ. And Jack approved and always complimented her on her taste and appearance. Two quick
Mary Benny examples: In London, at Claridge's,
Mary felt that the hotel's room-service charge for Perrier water was exorbitant, so she ordered a Rolls

Royce to drive her to a liquor store that advertised a sale on bottled waters. Example two: On one of the Benny trips to New York, Mary was robbed of a fortune in jewels by a burglar pretending to be a hotel bellboy. She was, quite understandably, shaken by the experience; but, after reporting the details to the police and explaining to Jack that she was unharmed, she hurried to Harry Winston (the world's most exclusive jeweler) and ordered a brand-new set of rings, necklaces, and bracelets. As she explained, it was like being thrown from a horse—one mustn't let any time elapse before getting back in the saddle. Mary proved that when the going gets tough, the tough go shopping.

The Benny parties were fun-oriented. Their guests were mostly old friends—and they had a gaggle of them. There was lots of show-business talk. Lots of "Will you ever forget when we had to follow Fink's mules at the Bijou in Altoona"; lots of "Let's all go to the hospital to visit Judy—she could use some cheering up"; lots of "If you think Danny is a pain in the ass, remember there'll never be anyone like Frank Fay." But there were very few requests for Jack to play his violin.

Sam Spiegel

Of all the parties, Sam's New Year's Eve gala was the most eagerly awaited. His pool area was tented over, caviar and champagne abounded, a name orchestra played, it started at eight with an enormous buffet and ended, for many, at breakfast on New Year's Day. Guests were allowed to bring their parents and their elsewhere-uninvited aunts and uncles. During the event literally hundreds of people arrived, stayed for a time, left, and often returned with another parcel of strays. As long as he lived, Sam continued to be the perfect host, courteous and gracious to one and all.

There was a small group who did not enjoy themselves as much. They were Sam's caterer/creditors, who often waited for payment until his next successful production. A man who felt money was essentially meant to bring enjoyment, Sam believed that others shouldn't worry about it any more than he did. Obviously he always paid his bills . . . often just in time to organize his next extravaganza.

His pictures included: *The Bridge on the River Kwai, Lawrence of Arabia, On the Waterfront,* and *The African Queen*. In his later years he spent most of his time on his oceangoing yacht—and I mean *yacht* —with his many friends, two Cordon Bleu chefs, and a lot of happy memories. But he often joked of the days when his money problems made it necessary to alter his name to S. P. Eagle . . . and when that wasn't enough for his creditors, to E. A. Gull.

Joan and Harry Cohn

Let me put it simply: Harry Cohn was not a beloved man. He was the primary owner and the absolute boss of Columbia Pictures. He chose, supervised, and made some of the best pictures ever and he also managed to make more enemies than anyone in town—no mean accomplishment, considering the competition. It is more likely fact than fiction that when a huge group of "mourners" turned out for his funeral, someone said, "See, if you give people what they want, they'll always show up." To paint the picture even more clearly, another "friend" claimed, "It isn't nice to speak ill of the dead, but in Harry's case I'll make an exception."

Cohn had an unerring ability to say the wrong thing

at the wrong time. At our first meeting he asked me if I enjoyed working for the Warners. I told him it was a wonderful experience. He answered, "Oh, you're another one of those guys who feel 'whose money I take, his song I sing.' " Our "friendship" began when I answered that there wasn't enough money in town to make me sing about him. The bad news? He thought that was a funny answer and I made a friend I didn't want.

Among his landmark comments: "How do I know when a picture is going to be a success? My ass tells me." Check his record—he must have had a very smart ass.

Joan Cohn—a charming and lovely woman—put up with a lot but never complained. She ran a beautiful home, beautifully, smiled a lot, sighed a lot, and enjoyed a more gentle life after Harry went to the Great Projection Room in the Sky and she married Laurence Harvey.

The Mason Ménage

A great deal of my adult bachelor life was spent in the company of James and Pamela Mason. They lived —and Pam still does—in one of Hollywood's true mansions, referred to by real estate agents as "the former Buster Keaton estate." Zsa Zsa Gabor introduced me to Mrs. Mason and I'll be forever grateful.

For some eight or nine years I headquartered with James and Pamela—so much so that a number of cynics weren't sure if the master or the mistress was the primary attraction. Shame on them for thinking in such terms. Both Masons were simply dear friends. With no conscious effort they managed to establish a grade-A collection of friends and passing-throughers.

It was at the Masons that I first met a lovely, sexy,

insecure young blonde named Marilyn Monroe. How insecure? So insecure that she glimpsed her image in a mirror and wanted to leave immediately because there was another blonde present who was wearing the same dress.

. . . and Joseph Mankiewicz, who had a lasting effect on me, not only because of his status as a multi-Oscar-winning producer/writer/director, but also because he ruined forever my newspaper-headline reading by pointing out that "mo*lester*" could just as properly be pronounced "*mole*ster." From now on you'll have that same problem.

. . . and Stewart Granger, who had to change his real name in motion pictures because he had been christened James Stewart and someone else in Hollywood had already made that name rather well known.

. . . and Ava Gardner—maybe the most beautiful lady of them all, who indicated some interest in me. I hurried her from the Masons to her apartment, where we spent several hours listening to the records of her true love, Artie Shaw. That wasn't exactly what I had in mind.

. . . and then Larry (now Lord) Olivier, who effusively complimented me on my "outstanding performance" opposite Joan Fontaine in *Frenchman's Creek,* and to this day he still thinks so, because I was too flattered (or chicken) to point out that it was Arturo de Cordova, not Fred, who was the Frenchman. (Arturo's last name was actually Ramos.)

. . . and Deborah Kerr, who confided in me that she was seriously considering going East to play the star role in *Tea and Sympathy* on the stage. I wisely explained to her that it would be a great mistake to leave the security of MGM for such a chancy undertaking. She rashly ignored my sage advice—and won every award the New York critics could bestow.

. . . and Richard Burton—just about the most

Fred and dear friend Pamela Mason.

charming man I've ever known—and his delightful wife at the time, Sybil. Burton was noted as a ladies' man, and it was said that none of his leading ladies had ever resisted his advances—or wanted to. But those of us who were close friends were well aware that, no matter how often he strayed, no one would ever cause a permanent breach between him and his loving and very understanding wife. When he was cast opposite Elizabeth Taylor in *Cleopatra,* there was gossip that their relationship was a serious one. I "knew" that it was just another Burton flirtation and made a thousand-dollar wager that when the picture was over he would bid Miss Taylor a charming good-bye and return, as always, to Sybil. You may have read that I made a slight thousand-dollar mistake.

James and Pamela Mason shared a unique marital arrangement—until they mutually decided that they had had enough of each other. They spent a large number of years together admiring and respecting each other without ever agreeing on any area of interest or manner of life-style. James was a devout introvert; Pam just the opposite. Each enjoyed different friends and different activities, but each believed that neither should presume to interfere with the other's activities. That was very adult and commendable, but it could be confusing to accept an invitation for dinner, only to find two totally different sets of guests in attendance: the James gang in one area of the living room discussing the futility of the government process and/or the styles of Truman Capote and Tennessee Williams; and the Pamela-ites grouped around the bar or television set gossiping about the latest escapades of the current studs and their "ladies-in-waiting." It was acceptable to move from one group to the other, but such an action could lead to a very muddled series of memories the next morning.

The Masons were generally scoffed at by the leading citizens of the community because of their lack of respect for the Establishment and the "laws of conduct." It was interesting to note, as time passed by and James's stature as a star increased, how so many, suddenly, found the Masons fascinating and their mode of conduct worthy of interest rather than absurdly bizarre and unacceptable.

Possibly the most disapproval was directed at the manner in which they raised their children. James and Pam believed that the most important factor in the mind of a child was the recognition that the parent was always in reach and concerned. Therefore, wherever they went, the children went with them—as infants, as babies, and as growing children. And when the time arrived that Portland and Morgan were growing up

223

enough to decide on their desires, their parents respected those decisions. By then they knew that closeness and loving care were available to them any hour of the day or night. It was the general consensus that, when they left the too-protective nest, the kids would go crazy.

Instead both grew up to be charming, respected, and successful. Morgan was for a time a Special Assistant to the President of the United States and now is the head man of his own public relations organization, and Portland is a published author. And each has remained devoted to Pamela and retained close ties with James even after they divorced and he established a new life, with a new wife, in Switzerland.

Morgan is my godson, Portland is a dear friend, and the Masons, no matter how unorthodox their parental-guidance program may have been, brought up two truly spectacular children. Which cannot in all instances be said for their more conventional contemporaries. Today Pamela, Portland, and Morgan—with James's wishes, I'm sure—constitute a solid parent-child relationship that could be a model for all families. And they did it the old-fashioned way—they earned it.

You Can Count
Your Friends . . .

I have been told that, at seventy-six, I have finally reached the stage in life where people enjoy:

Music of the Forties
Driving in the Fifties
Women in their Sixties
Temperature in the Seventies
Golf in the Eighties
Friends in their Nineties

A good deal of that is true. Actually, *all* of it is true, if you'll agree to lower the numbers in the "friend area" a trifle.

Obviously, at one time my friends were not as old as they are now. Many of them were quite young—but that was a long time ago. A lot of folks who were near and dear to me are, because of funeral services, no longer available to me, and I regret that on a regular basis. We spent some memorable times together, and I miss them.

I found Ernie Kovacs bigger than life and better than most, even before he became a comedy legend.

He was a gambling man, but if he'd gambled more on a certain night, he might be here today. That night I held good cards and blitzed him six games in a row at gin. I offered to play him another game, double or nothing, but he declined, saying it wasn't his lucky night. He was right. He left the game, wrapped his station wagon around a lamppost, and left a drearier world behind. He also left a widow who worked more than "overtime" to pay off the fortune in gambling debts he'd incurred. Edie Adams paid off every dime.

Alfred Bloomingdale—Mr. Department Store and Mr. Diners Club—was, for a bunch of years, my closest friend. Three times I was his best man at his marriages and have the engraved watches to prove it. I worked for, and with, him when he forayed into show business in New York, met my wife at his beachfront home in California, introduced him to Betsy Newling, and became the godfather of two of their three children. It was a genuine pleasure to spend as much time as I did with such a happily married couple. When Alfred died, the Vicki Morgan story broke, and I still can't convince people that, close as Al and I were, I never had an inkling that "another woman" existed. I have a feeling that Betts and I were the only two who didn't know.

I miss the Thin Man—Bill Powell. They said if you looked up the word *gentleman* in the dictionary, you'd find his picture. During his declining—in health only —years, he lived in Palm Springs, lovingly looked after by his charming wife, Mousie. His big outings were twice-a-day visits to his mailbox, and his social gatherings were few but very special to those involved. He spent most of his time reading biographies (he knew every detail about everyone) and watching television, which he alternately blessed and damned. When his chums came to the desert and phoned The Mouse to check on his availability, it was wonderful to hear that Daddy was feeling fine and was looking forward to seeing us "on Wednesday, for cocktails and talk." Jack Lemmon, who co-starred with Bill in *Mr. Roberts* (and won an Oscar as Ensign Pulver), and I always saved time for and savored every moment of our visits with the Powells when we were in the Springs to play golf in the Bob Hope Classic. The evenings were essentially the same: Mrs. Powell would meet us at the door; Bill, waiting in the study, would be "casually" dressed in silk pajamas and matching robe. Beside him, there would be a photo album of his friends and stills from his movies, chilled martinis would be available, and we'd talk of the people in the album, remind each other of days and nights spent together, and enjoy his memories and anecdotes. Each year there would be fewer photos of remaining friends, and finally there were no pictures and no Bill Powell. Mousie still invites Lemmon and me to drop in for cocktails. We do, but she'll be the first to understand, it isn't the same.

If you're a close friend of Frank Sinatra's, you live in a special world. Your life is filled with happy events and some surprises. If Frank doesn't like you, the town—whatever town—may not be big enough for the two of you. And you can be sure *he* isn't leaving.

I don't think there's ever been a bigger spender, a more lavish gift giver, a more "but-don't-mention-my-name" charity donor, a softer touch, a better audience for another performer, a more loyal friend, or a man who can switch more quickly to a belligerent adversary in the middle of a relaxed and friendly conversation than Ol' Blue Eyes.

What is it like spending time with him? Well, you're dining with him and a few of his friends at the Sinatra complex in Palm Springs—he thinks it might be fun to try the tables in Vegas—he phones the airport and orders his plane to ready up—limos drive you onto

The Sinatras and the de Cordovas. We got a good table.

the tarmac—on board there's champagne and Jack Daniel's waiting for you. In Las Vegas more limos show up and the group is escorted to the tables. Everyone gambles—Frank has a lucky streak—if you weren't as lucky, he pays off what you lost. I keep telling him the reason I was in Palm Springs was to play in a golf tournament and I'm scheduled to tee off at eight in the morning. He tells me not to worry. At 5:30 A.M. I mention my problem again—he makes a phone call or two—we arrive back in Palm Springs at 7:00—his man is at the airport with my golf clubs and shoes—there's a 'copter warming up—I'm dropped off at the first tee at 7:30 and the pilot hands me a dozen golf balls, "courtesy of Mr. Sinatra."

I've known Nancy, the first Mrs. Sinatra, and Ava, Mia, and Barbara. Each speaks highly of him. I've known all his children, and they love him dearly. So do I—but I've seen him turn into a holy terror, and it wasn't a pretty sight to behold. In fairness, I haven't seen that happen in the last few years. In equal fairness, I haven't been on his "we're-looking-forward-to-seeing-you-on-Thursday" list in the last few years. I assume it's an oversight.

Janet and I are blessed indeed, friendship-wise. You can't be more blessed if you are on Veronique and Gregory Peck's "good list." They have a gorgeous home, everyone loves them and the parties they give, their children are polite and attractive, and as a family, they give the town an image it can be proud of—and is. Veronique is beautiful, well traveled, and a wonderful conversationalist; but my close relationship with Greg is unique. Every time I see him, I ask him to make an appearance on *The Tonight Show*. He invariably answers, "That's rather unlikely." I then ask him if that means "no." He then explains that "no" would be a rude answer to a friend, but that "unlikely" means exactly the same—with an escape hatch. I've taken to using "unlikely" a good deal recently.

I have more success with the man who is probably the last remaining major motion-picture star of the Golden Days of Hollywood—Jimmy Stewart. If you've starred with Garbo, Hepburn, Jean Arthur, Margaret Sullavan, Duke Wayne, Dietrich, and a rabbit named Harvey, you really were there when there was a "there."

Jimmy comes on our show two or three times a year, and it's an "occasion." The moment he's introduced he receives the standing ovation he deserves as a star and as a person. No one has served his country and the motion-picture industry as well. He's aware of what he's done, he's pleased with his success, he's proud of his children, and there isn't a pretentious bone in his very tall body. Add to that a world-class wife.

Gloria invented a wonderful family game to stop her children from name-dropping. When anyone at the dinner table showed off by mentioning a star they'd run into that day, Gloria would stamp her feet à la Sammy Davis, Jr. The game became a part of the conversational pattern. One night Jimmy was irked by a Gloria remark and said, "Gloria, that's just ridiculous, for Christ's sake." And the entire family started stomping.

One more sidelight: Gloria and Jimmy live in the most exclusive section of Beverly Hills, but they felt a little hemmed in. So they bought the house next door to them, tore it down, and planted a vegetable garden —which they tend. Jimmy says he loves to garden, even if each ear of corn costs him about sixteen dollars.

One's friends are a rather mixed bag, and that's as it should be. If you choose "truly good," you can spend time with Pat Boone and try to find out if he's as decent and upstanding as he seems to be. Save the effort—he is. And if you aren't as close a friend of God's as he is, he doesn't hold it against you.

Janet and I enjoy being with Zsa Zsa and Eva Gabor —when they are friendly. And even more when they are not. Their husbands and their dalliances have, however, made a looseleaf address book a necessity.

Cubby and Dana Broccoli live in the mansion that Bill Powell built for Jean Harlow but don't spend all of their time discussing who will be the next "007" in their super-successful James Bond movies. Two of their closest friends are Sean Connery and Roger Moore—and why not? All have grown rich together. Plus Cubby has the decency to spend his money properly. One Christmas a New York friend of his mentioned that he missed the feel of the season, the snow in particular. The Broccolis gave a party for the friend and arranged to have their lawn and driveway covered

Zsa Zsa Gabor, Fred MacMurray and the director of "My Three Sons" plan the next setup.

with man-made snow. Sleighs met the guests at the gate. After all, what are friends for!

William Peter Blatty wrote *The Exorcist,* made a fortune, and bought the largest and most unusual house on the beach at Malibu. Evenings at his home were slightly different from the usual. After a normal, conventional cocktail hour and dinner, his guests were regularly invited to listen to tapes and recordings of conversations from outer space. Bill was much luckier than his guests: he had no trouble at all hearing and understanding what the extraterrestrials were saying. I quickly learned that the quicker you managed to hear what he was hearing, the less likely you were to be asked to "listen closely, I'm sure you'll understand them this time."

Fred and June Haver MacMurray give marriage and Hollywood a good name. No charitable request—for money or a personal appearance—is refused by them. But Fred, one of the wealthiest men in the community, has a reputation as one of its most reluctant spenders. It is said—apocryphally, I'm sure—that Fred and Cary Grant met for dinner one evening, the check was placed halfway between them, and it was ignored by both of them for so long that the waiter finally asked them if they were ready to order breakfast. People say that "care for a buck" stems from a childhood when every penny was precious and "waste not want not" was the family creed. Apparently, what Fred learned as a child remained in him as an adult.

X-Rated

Not all of our friends are so middle of the road. Sidney Chaplin, whose father was a rather successful comedian, is funny himself, but he is, shall we say, forthright in his speech. He has had considerable success on stage and in bed, he's certainly handsome, but he's been known to cause a problem. Example—his bawdy conversation in a Palm Springs restaurant caused a nearby diner to rise from his table and address Sidney sternly: "Young man, please watch your language. I happen to be sitting with my fiancée." Sidney pointed to the lady sitting with him and calmly asked, "What do you think this girl is, a bucket of shit?" Sidney has a master's degree in room-clearing.

More prosaically, we have good times with the tightly knit group of the Michael Caines and Louis Jourdans and Roger Moores; with the Kirk Douglases and Bob Newharts and Don Rickleses and a batch of others, who are as remarkable for what they are as for what they've done. But most of all, Janet and I look forward to the times we spend with the two couples who are nearest and dearest to us: the Billy Wilders and the Irving Lazars.

It is unfortunate that, at this point in time, Mr. Wilder and Mr. Lazar are something less than buddies, although for many years they were closer than close. Both of them are, in my opinion, losers thereby. Janet and I love them all, individually or in any form of packaging, and wish we could alter the four-pack into the six-pack it used to be.

A lot of nice things have been written about the Wilders and the Lazars—deservedly so. They are fascinating people and I'm not sure I can do them justice, but I'll try. They are, to start with, just about the best at what they do—and what they say about what they do.

The Billy Wilders

Billy: Born in Austria in 1906. Newspaperman. To Hollywood in 1934 after working on a screenplay for UFA.

PICTURES INCLUDE:

(writer)	*Ninotchka*
	Arise My Love
	Ball of Fire
	Hold Back the Dawn
(director/writer)	*The Major and the Minor*
	Five Graves to Cairo
	Double Indemnity
	Lost Weekend
	Sunset Boulevard
	Big Carnival
	Stalag 17

(director/writer)   *Sabrina*
Love in the Afternoon
Some Like It Hot
The Apartment
Irma La Douce
Seven Year Itch
Spirit of St. Louis
Fortune Cookie

Multi-Academy Award winner, Director's Guild Award winner, American Film Institute honoree, recognized art expert, acknowledged humorist, sports expert, and aficionado, proud American, foe of sham in government and moviemaking, gourmet—and friend of mine. Who could ask for anything more?

Billy Wilder, forget about his career if you can, may be the wittiest, on the spur of the moment, man I have ever known. Who else when asked to compare his talents with those of Willie Wyler (another directorial giant) would answer: "Wyler, Wilder? Manet, Monet!"

Billy is intolerant of bureaucracy and whatever political party is in power. He suffers these days with a bad back and has visited so many doctors that he refers to them by number, not by name. Food is important to him, and Audrey, his wife, is not only beautiful but also the best cook in town. It is unlikely that any place except a museum—and not all of them—can match the paintings and the sculptures hung and placed haphazardly throughout the Wilder apartment.

Billy's interest in baseball and football is enormous. He hopes that when he dies it will be after the World Series and the Super Bowl—following that, there isn't much in life to look forward to . . . till next year.

It's my personal belief that he'd like to be more active than he is, picture-wise, and I feel the industry would be the better for it if he were.

Close friends: Audrey and Billy Wilder.

Mr. and Mrs. Swifty

Let's wrap it up with Mary and Irving Lazar and point out a few parallels with Janet and Fred de Cordova. Irving, who doesn't approve of being called "Swifty" any more than Bill Shoemaker likes "Willie," stayed single until he was fifty-six. I made the momentous marriage move when I was fifty-three. The Lazars live in a splendid home on the same street as, and almost directly opposite, the de Cordovas. If that isn't enough togetherness, Irving used to "go" with Janet. I didn't "go" with Mary—but I'd have been glad to.

In passing, I did "go" with Audrey Young before she married Billy Wilder. No, Billy didn't "go" with any of us.

If Irving Lazar had his way, he would never be home except for the required few hours of sleep each night. He delights in lunch with "chums," cocktailing with "my very dear friends," and hosting perfectly planned small dinner parties. He would like to play golf better than he does, he has tickets—and goes—to all Dodger and Ram home games, and he manages to stay in touch at least once a day or night—by phone or in person—with every client he represents. He is a dynamo.

He has an apartment in New York and selected hotel suites in all the European capitals and resorts. He loves to keep moving—can't stand being in one place when there's a "happening" in another. He's remarkable and so is Mary. She manages to ramrod her husband's activities, sees that he's properly packed and pilled, runs the house and apartment impeccably, looks like a doll, and somehow manages to find time to run her own extremely active business interests.

Close friends: Mary and Irving Lazar.

Mr. Lazar, not the easiest man to fit, has more suits in his closet than he'll ever be able to wear. He can't stand dirt or dust and washes and showers before and after he does anything. His client list is a who's who of authors and he reads "every word they write." Which, of course, is impossible—in addition to unlikely. Even so, the books of these clients are invariably sold to publishers and wind up on the best-seller list—so *somebody* reads them. I might add here that he is given to obvious exaggeration and then fools you by being accurate.

Swifty (sorry, I can't keep writing "Mr. Lazar") is as prolific a spender as you'll ever meet. But he's no fool. He is willing to pay the going price for the best —but it has to be just that.

The Lazar Oscar Night party for almost two hundred people—held for the past two years at L.A.'s trendy Spago restaurant—is, regularly, the toughest ticket in town. From year to year the guest list is revised, those who were rude or troublesome are eliminated, rising stars and newcomers with charm are added, and from the day the invitations are mailed, Mary and Irving are inundated by "I hope we'll be included." Sure it's nice to be Oscar-nominated, but the Lazar party is a nomination in itself. And you could make a movie for about the same cost.

In this climate fast friendships are quickly forgotten when the box-office reports show red, but the Lazars are constant and loyal. Their friendship isn't built on your most recent success . . . or failure.

Irving is as at ease with Guy de Rothschild as he is with Tommy Lasorda, with Gloria Vanderbilt as with Kareem Abdul-Jabbar, with Oscar de la Renta as with Marvelous Marvin Hagler. You're liable to find them all at the Lazars on a given night, and somehow, at the end of the festivities, everyone will have had a fine time, all will be pleased with their new friends, and no one will have felt out of place. On the *very* rare occasions when the mix doesn't work too well and staring matches replace sparkling conversations, it is reassuring to remember that I live right across the street and an unnoticed exit can be made with no one the wiser.

I have an added area of authority in the Lazar legend. Not just because we see a good deal of each other on both coasts and agree, in the main, on most people and projects, but also because Irving and I spent a month together in Africa. I was with him as we flew into Nairobi, where he managed to leave his money and credit cards on the plane. I photographed him as he bravely patted the horn of a rhino, I helped him onto (and quickly off of) a skittish giraffe, I chased after him as he ran in circles because a baboon jumped from a tree and landed in the center of Irving's washbasin. I stood nearby when a tribe of Masai warriors took photos of *him*. And I was there when he made a hole in one on the golf course at Bill Holden's deluxe Mt. Kenya Resort and Game Reserve. A lucky bounce off the rear end of a panicked peacock.

Forget the Oscar party, forget Irving's status as a super agent, forget his wisdom and his wit. I know the man under all circumstances: on a scale of ten, he's a ten.

Johnny—in costume—welcomes me back from the Lazar–de Cordova African safari.

Afterword

Say Goodnight,
Freddie

The passing years bring with them a great number of disadvantages—death being one of the most hazardous. Only slightly less depressing are the increasing requests to compare The Old Days with The Nowadays. Was The Past more fun than The Present? Was it more glamorous? More exciting? And if it was, why?

A famous songwriter, Abe Burrows, once wrote a comedy ballad entitled: "I'm Traveling Down Memory Lane Without a Goddam Thing to Remember." I don't suffer from that problem: every day I'm reminded of something that happened a long time ago. I have an understandable reluctance to pay much attention to the passage of time, and a certain animosity toward those who assume that if one is in his seventies he must have been a high school buddy of Abraham Lincoln. It's a dubious compliment to be considered just enough this side of senility to recall a few names and places that "Mother and Dad said you were the one person who'd remember."

There's a danger in playing the "yes-indeed-I'll-never-forget-the-night" game. If I am the only one who was there, there's a strong temptation to add a little verbal polish to what really happened and to eliminate some of the less exciting moments. After all, Then and Now are nothing more than a series of episodes in an ongoing soap opera, peopled by an ever-changing cast of characters—with the changes not always for the better, or the worse. Let me explain: My only beef with the march of time is that it has eliminated many too many of the people I'd like to have available to me to verify my memories—and my evaluations.

It is both simple and stupid to insist that What Was is clearly superior to What Is. It is understandable, however, to feel that what we did a long time ago was probably considerably more exciting than what we did last Thursday night. There is, after all, the Law of Diminishing Returns.

Granted I was There, and I am Here, and it is my intention to compare, objectively, the good old days with these very good days. I'll try to explain why I enjoyed myself as much as I did and why I'm still having such a good time. I'll try to evaluate the contributing factors as I go along, and I hope you'll come to a decision—along with me.

Let's open with an acknowledgment that nostalgia should be recognized for the monster it is—a state of excessive yearning, an attitude based on sentiment—and let's agree that we're going to sidestep that trap. As I promised, we're going to be objective.

I will admit I'm constantly upset that everything costs an unacceptable amount more than it used to—the price of a shoe shine or a bottle of beer, a shirt or a hotel room, a cup of coffee or an automobile, and, more pertinent to the business I'm in, the price of admission to a movie or a Broadway theater. But I'm smart enough to realize that if everything costs ten times as much as it used to, our salaries are ten times as large as they were. Dedicated as I am to a dollar, cost of living will not enter into my evaluation.

An enormous amount of drivel, and some truth, has been written about the glamour of Hollywood in the Golden Days, as opposed to the more mundane style of today. The legend persists—or is it a legend?—that social events were more exciting, more exotic, than they are now, that the guests in attendance were less inhibited, their personas more electric.

One's age at the time and one's exposure to star-studded bashes can clearly color one's judgment, as must the recognition that at one period in time the big names were *movie* stars, while today most of the celebrities emerge from your friendly television set. Just a comment, not a judgment.

Remember that during the halcyon days of the Big Screen, most of the stars played only two or three roles per year and made only a few highly publicized "personal appearances" (one of the most self-aggrandizing phrases ever invented). You saw them on the screen and that was it. Their publicity people made sure that you realized their lives were light-years away from yours. The condescending ads indicating that a June Allyson or a Judy Garland was "just like the girl next door" were a prime example. The studio plan was to widen as much as possible the gap between the movie star and the movie goer. And it worked.

You should realize that with a few exceptions (there are idiots in all generations), the subjects of all this idolatry were intelligent enough to recognize the hoop-la for the hogwash it was. They understood that the glamorizing process was a vital cog in insuring their status and longevity, box-office-wise. They realized that any, even casual, relationship would be described as a "passionate affair," any travel would be a "pilgrimage," their homes would be "mansions" or "estates," their children would be "heirs apparent," and it would be implicit that they had no knowledge of, or any use for, bathroom facilities.

As a matter of fact, very few of these idols had been discovered at soda fountains or gas stations. Many had spent years on the stage, and, believe it or not, some even had college degrees.

Forget their backgrounds, they were special people. It is pure delight when I remember the fun of having a drink with Gable, telling a joke and being rewarded by Cooper's slow smile, having Flynn whisper "Drop by my place after the party breaks up," sitting on a piano bench with Crosby while he noodled and sang, dancing with a lovely lady who turned out to be Lana Turner, being told there was a seat open for poker at Betty Grable's house, going to a football game with Bob Taylor and Barbara Stanwyck, golfing with Hope, swimming with Esther Williams, or spending a Palm Springs weekend with the Bennys and Dinah Shore.

Wait a minute, it's not a one-way street. There are a lot of extremely impressive movie stars around today. How about Redford and Nicholson, Newman and Stallone, Burt Reynolds, Dustin Hoffman, Streep and Lange and Sally Field, Streisand, De Niro, Pacino, Goldie Hawn, Woody Allen and Jane Fonda, Lemmon and Matthau? They are, let's agree, just as talented and attractive as their earlier counterparts. I promised to be completely honest with you, so I have to admit I've never met Redford or Streep—but nobody's perfect, I never met Spencer Tracy, either.

Today we are blessed with the world of TV. It and you have created a new and different category of superstars. They are infinitely closer to you, their fans, because they come to call on a regular basis in your living rooms, your dens, your bedrooms. They are available at every hour of the day and night, and if they don't pleasure you at the moment, you don't have

Bill Holden, Bob Hope and I discuss our scores after the day's golf at the Hope Classic.

Actor/director Fred de Cordova with real actor Tony Randall and real director Martin Scorsese on the set of *The King of Comedy*.

to go out into the cold, find your car, and drive all the way home. A twist of the dial takes care of the problem. If they don't pleasure you at all, relax—there'll be a whole new batch next season.

There's quite an impressive group who have entertained you via the tube: Cosby and Carson, Letterman and Selleck, Don Johnson, Linda Evans and Joan Collins, Peter Falk, Michael Landon, Tyne Daly and Sharon Gless, John Forsythe, Angela Lansbury, Newhart, plus Brokaw, Rather, and Peter Jennings. Nobody's listening—you can admit how much they have entertained you.

No, I haven't forgotten the music world. You loved Jolson, now try Iglesias. Caruso, there's Pavarotti. Billie Holiday, Streisand. And we had, and still have, Tony Bennett, Andy Williams, Steve and Eydie, Lena Horne, Mel Tormé, and Ol' Blue Eyes—all of them better than ever. If you don't believe me, ask them.

At this juncture, it seems that what we Had and what we Have are running pretty much neck and neck. So let's try another area of comparison: let's move from people to places and things.

Let's assume that everyone we've mentioned is, or was, decent and honest, moral and charitable, loyal and patriotic, sincere and loving—and extremely fond of you. Unlikely though it may be, let's suppose that not even one of these big shots is giving a dinner party tonight—or if they are, you weren't invited. You now have to decide where to go for dinner.

First, you thank your favorite God that this isn't one of those nights when some professional philanthropist or some popular disease is being honored in a drafty hotel ballroom with tickets going for a minimum of a hundred dollars a copy. As a result, you will miss being seated, along with several strangers, at a front table where you would be able to watch, at close range, the eating and drinking habits of the honored

guests on the dais. You'll also miss the endless introductions of all the committee members who "really
made this evening possible" while you gnaw on the
cold roast beef that was preceded by the salmon-less
mousse. You will never know how much, to the
penny, was raised by the ads in the program or how
large is the debt owed to the perfume company that
has placed one-third-of-an-ounce bottles of aftershave in front of, oddly enough, all the ladies. You
will not have to wait an hour for your car to be retrieved from the rear of the hotel garage, nor will you
notice, until you get home, the sizable dent in your
right-rear fender. Which your wife will imply was
there before you left for the Gala.

None of the above—you'll just go to a restaurant. I
am sure that many of you are gourmets; but I am not.
I settle, quickly, for almost any eating establishment
that features fast service, moderate prices, sincere
drinks, a menu printed in English, and comfortable
seating. We all realize that the fun of a dinner out is
really determined by the people with you—plus one
dear soul who can be counted on to say: "I've had a
great time, but I have to get up early in the morning."
That's a pal. An enemy is the man or woman who
insists: "It's only eleven—wouldn't everyone like an
after-dinner drink?"

Okay, I'm easy to please; not everyone is. Choosing
a restaurant becomes a ritual. Everyone has a favorite:

1. "They always seem to be pleased to see us."
2. "Just about everyone goes there."
3. "It's almost like being in Italy."
4. "It's very reasonable, if you compare it."
5. "Don't worry about the tab, I own a piece of the
place."

I dine out three or four times a week and have done

so ever since I can remember. I have enjoyed myself, or not, in all the grade-A restaurants for over fifty years. Next to eating at home, these were the best:

Then

ROMANOFF'S . . . because
Bogart and Bacall would be there. The Masons and Richard Burton, too. Probably Groucho. Good food, generous drinks. If you were a little "short," Mike remembered when he had suffered from the same dread disease, and "carried" you.

LA RUE
The elegant restaurant. Ladies really dressed up to go there—Roz Russell, Greer Garson, Norma Shearer. Emphasis on wines and sauces. Very MGM-y. Red, the best bartender ever—by the time you opened your napkin, your favorite drink arrived. One block from Mocambo, if you wanted to go on and dance. People did in those days. Even me.

PERINO'S
Numero Uno. They invented ambiance. On your way downtown to the theater—still open on your way back. Financed by the owners of the *Los Angeles Times* so that the "community would have one fine restaurant." I don't think it ever broke even. But not to worry—the *Times* has a big circulation.

THE LUAU
Polynesian food and drink and decor. Two of their rum drinks and no one cared about the food or the beaded curtains. Nondrinkers were tolerated and

probably enjoyed the egg rolls. On Rodeo Drive, it was torn down to make room for chic and exclusive boutiques. Not every change is for the better.

DOMINICK'S

Unique. Dom owned it and bartended. Peggy, his wife, cooked. Niece Addie was the waitress. The jukebox contained only Sinatra records. Very limited food selection—all great. If Dom liked you, no reservation was necessary. If he didn't, you couldn't get in—even if no one else showed up.

CHASEN'S

Opened by Dave as a chili bar. Caught on fast and became "21" in L.A. Best simple fare in the world. The Jimmy Stewarts, Alfred Hitchcock, the Greg Pecks. Young Ronnie Reagan liked it, too.

Now

CHASEN'S

See directly above. Dave's widow, Maude, runs it now. Pepe's martinis very special. The staff never changes—nor the clientele. President Reagan's first choice. Mine, too.

SPAGO

The new kid in town and *the* place to go. Every night is New Year's Eve. Chief cook and owner Wolfgang Puck has made pizza respectable food. His wife, Barbara Lazaroff, in charge of welcomes and hugs. In likely attendance: Johnny Carson and Joan Rivers (not at same table), Tom Selleck, Angie Dickinson, Arnold Schwarzenegger, Cher, Dudley Moore, Wilders and Lazars (not at same table). Fun is featured here.

Dave Chasen as a "stooge" for Joe Cook in *Hold Your Horses* in 1933. He looked a bit different as the owner of Chasen's Restaurant.

MORTON'S

Noisy but nice. See the studio heads, their top stars, and the agents who put the deal together all acting like friends. You'll enjoy the food, but won't be able to hear what anyone is saying—not the worst thing in the world. Young stars go there, too, and wow, do they look young!

THE BISTRO

Now's version of La Rue. Show your out-of-town friends that pretty ladies still dress properly. Bring your bankroll. You'll be well fed and treated nicely. Great spot to take your wife to indicate how highly you still regard her.

And there are all the other spots your friends prefer to the ones I've mentioned. Every kind of food, every kind of atmosphere, every kind of clientele. But wasn't it always so?

There *were* fine hotels and there *are* fine hotels. We took trains and they got us there, we take planes and they get us there faster, but maybe a tad less pleasantly. There are more golf courses and tennis courts than there used to be, but you can play on only one at a time. We have air-conditioning, but we seem to have more colds. Women were beautiful and they still are, but infidelity is rampant. Doctors cure diseases and new ones develop. Autos go faster and we have a 55-mile-per-hour speed limit. Computers are invented and it's impossible to correct a mistake the computer made. Television has brought the world together and shows us daily how much people hate one another. We end one war with an atomic bomb and live in its shadow from that day on. So *was* it better or *is* it better? I'll be back in a minute with my verdict.

The Envelope, Please

I've thought it over carefully and I've made my decision. After due deliberation, and at the recognized risk of being considered an old fogy, I've chosen the Past, when slower clocks struck happier hours. It's not, I assure you, that I must vote for bygone days because my future is past. No way. My deal with Johnny reads that as long as he hosts *The Tonight Show,* I'll be the executive producer. That means we'll both face every day "turned on" by the challenges and the options of the show that night. We'll continue to search for the new and bright young funny men and women, we'll enjoy finding the most attractive young actresses, we'll uncover the interesting performers who have something to say and know how to say it amusingly; we'll keep on looking for the senior citizens who have managed to keep their heads above water and retained a joy in living and an ability to tell us why. We'll welcome showing up at 11:30 "on most of these stations," and, along with Ed and Doc, we'll get well paid for enjoying ourselves as much as we have for the last million years.

That's just the working-hours side of the coin. There's also the department of health and welfare. I seem to have successfully broken all the rules that apply to sensible people. My personal rule number one is: Never be stupid enough to visit a doctor or surgeon. That will keep you from worrying about a disease you don't know you have. I am a firm believer in the axiom that a hospital is no place for a sick person.

My private life seems to be in working order, too. I enjoy, immensely, the afternoons and evenings I spend with the friends I've had over the years, and

Janet and Fred in a current phase.

expect to continue that enjoyment well into the future —if they are decent enough to remain alive. And, from time to time, I meet someone new who is amusing and knowledgeable—even if he or she suffers from Youth.

Self-indulgently, as if in an award-winning acceptance speech, I'd like to pay a special tribute to my wife. Janet is beautiful and supportive, and we share more regard and love than most people are entitled to. And we have an agreement that so long as we both shall live, we will continue our search for a subject on which we agree.

After rereading the last few paragraphs—my work, my health, my friends, and my married life—I'm not so sure of my earlier decision. The past, the present, and the future may wind up in a flat-footed tie. One thing is sure: I'm a very lucky man.

These words are being written late at night, I'm a little weary, my brandy glass is empty, my cigarette supply is running low, I tee off early in the morning, and the show is all booked for next week. This seems to be the proper time to thank you for traveling this far in the life of a very happy man. By so doing, you've made me even happier.

Postscript

December 1989

I am not the first to recognize that as time goes by, so much changes—and so much stays the same. The hardcover edition of *Johnny Came Lately* appeared ("exploded" might be an overstatement) in March of 1988. This softcover edition is due to be in your favorite bookstore in December of 1989. What, you ask, has the passage of a year and nine months done to me, to Johnny Carson, and to those near to him and to me? Let me list the ways.

Many of the pretenders to the late-night television throne—Joan Rivers, the Wilton North Report, and David Brenner, to mention a trio—have thrown in their talk-show towels. Two new challengers—Pat Sajak and Arsenio Hall—have appeared on the scene. Both of these nice young men and their programs have followed the exact same pattern as those who preceded them: a large flurry of publicity indicating that the time may be at hand to topple King Carson from his throne; acceptable ratings during their first month or so as competitors; and then the same old refrain—

Carson solidly on top, Koppel and his version of the nightly news in second place, and a battle between the newcomers for the viewers who are left.

Garry Shandling, for whom I have high regard, opted to concentrate his television activities on his own comedy program, and, as a result, Jay Leno became the sole guest host of *The Tonight Show*. He has become a resounding success and is, I believe, well on his way to lasting, and deserved, importance in the field of comedy.

Johnny and NBC have agreed to continue their happy relationship until, at least, September of 1990, and most of us who are part of *The Tonight Show* family are delighted, because we've been "included in" for that period of time.

One notable exception. Henry Bushkin and Johnny came to a parting of the ways, primarily, it seems, because of Bushkin's desire to expand the Carson Company's television activities and Johnny's desire to concentrate his focus on his primary interest, *The Tonight Show*. Ed Hookstratten, a major legal figure in the entertainment world, now guides the Carson activities.

Ed McMahon, Doc Severinsen, Peter Lassally, Bobby Quinn, and most of the writing staff plus the talented Talent Coordinators are still aboard ship and extremely happy to be there.

On a purely personal note, *Johnny Came Lately* opened up a truly wonderful and brand-new world to me. From March 14, 1988, when the Irving Lazars invited all of Hollywood to a book-unveiling at Spago (and an amazing number of luminaries actually showed up), I have had a wonderful time on "the book tour" explaining on television, radio, and to newspaper editors and book reviewers why readers would have the time of their lives if they bought and read *Johnny Came Lately*.

On ninety-eight occasions, I met the public via the media in one fashion or another and learned over and over again just how much of an impact *The Tonight Show* (and Johnny Carson) has had on the lives of the viewing public.

I also learned from a surprisingly large number of readers that I had misspelled "Mad Dog" Coll's name and that Simon and Schuster and I had captioned a photo of David Wolper presenting me an Emmy as Daniel Wolper. He has forgiven me; I hope you do.

I'm extremely happy, though it's none of my business, to report that the Carsons—Alex and Johnny—appear to be even happier than ever. And that Janet and I continue, amicably, our search for a subject we can agree on.

All of us have been saddened by the too-many friends who have left us. Lucille Ball, Gilda Radner, and Ruth (Mrs. Milton) Berle will be sorely missed. But we are heartened that George Burns and Bob Hope defy the odds and continue to charm us, on stage and off.

And, at the risk of being much too self-serving, I am absolutely delighted that I'm still here and still doing *The Tonight Show*.

Index